A Business Guide to
Information Security

How to protect your company's IT assets, reduce risks and understand the law

Alan Calder

RECOMMENDED BY
INSTITUTE OF DIRECTORS

KOGAN
PAGE
London and Sterling, VA

This book has been endorsed by the Institute of Directors.

The endorsement is given to selected Kogan Page books which the IoD recognizes as being of specific interest to its members and providing them with up-to-date, informative and practical resources for creating business success. Kogan Page books endorsed by the IoD represent the most authoritative guidance available on a wide range of subjects including management, finance, marketing, training and HR.

The views expressed in this book are those of the author and are not necessarily the same as those of the Institute of Directors.

Publisher's note

Every possible effort has been made to ensure that the information contained in this book is accurate at the time of going to press, and the publishers and author cannot accept responsibility for any errors or omissions, however caused. No responsibility for loss or damage occasioned to any person acting, or refraining from action, as a result of the material in this publication can be accepted by the editor, the publisher or the author.

First published in Great Britain and the United States in 2005 by Kogan Page Limited

120 Pentonville Road
London N1 9JN
United Kingdom
www.kogan-page.co.uk

22883 Quicksilver Drive
Sterling VA 20166-2012
USA

© Alan Calder, 2005

The right of Alan Calder to be identified as the author of this work has been asserted by him in accordance with the Copyright, Designs and Patents Act 1988.

ISBN 0 7494 4395 2

British Library Cataloguing-in-Publication Data

A CIP record for this book is available from the British Library.

Library of Congress Cataloging-in-Publication Data

Calder, Alan, 1957–
  A business guide to information security : how to protect your
company's IT assets, reduce risks and understand the law / Alan Calder.
    p. cm.
  Includes index.
  ISBN 0-7494-4395-2
  1. Computer security. 2. Information technology—Security measures.
3. Data protection. 4. Business—Data processing—Security measures. I. Title.
QA76.9.A25C34188 2005
005.8—dc22   2005019163

Typeset by JS Typesetting Ltd, Porthcawl, Mid Glamorgan
Printed and bound in Great Britain by Creative Print and Design (Wales), Ebbw Vale

Contents

About the author

Alan Calder, founder director of IT Governance Ltd, led one of the first organizations to achieve BS7799. His 30-year international management career, at CEO and director level in both the private and public sectors, has increasingly focused on the challenge of making information security as simple and as natural as household security. He is the author of *IT Governance* and *Corporate Governance* (both published by Kogan Page).

How to use this book

ANALOGUE AND DIGITAL

This book was designed, and is intended to be used, as both a **digital** and an **analogue** (that is, dual online and hardcopy) resource. The speed of evolution in computing and of the **internet** means that any book on **information security** starts going out of date fairly quickly. On top of that, there is a six- to eight-month gap between completing the text for and the publication of a hard-covered book. This inevitably means that many technologies that were new, new-ish but inadequately tested, or still only dreams at the point I completed the text could not be included in the analogue version of this book. The reader should therefore assume, from the outset, that the KnowledgeBank at www.itgovernance.co.uk is essential and should use it on a regular basis in order to access the most current information on the issues covered in this book.

The updated information is available only to people who have purchased a hardcopy of the book and can be accessed by going to the **subscriber intranet** at www.itgovernance.co.uk and typing the unique user number that is supplied on the back of this book into the logon box. This will enable the reader to access a free six-month subscription to the KnowledgeBank **update services**, of the website, with a low cost option to renew thereafter.

The reader is also able to assess a number of additional services, including information, alert services and mentoring services that are designed to help readers of the book tackle information security issues. A full set of templates, that are compatible with the advice to businesses in this book and also capable of being deployed in an **ISO 17799** or **BS 7799 ISMS** are also accessible through the website. Full information is available on www.itgovernance.co.uk.

WHAT, AND WHY, NOT HOW?

This book tells you *what* you need to do – or ensure you have done – to secure your information systems and **assets**. It also tells you *why* you need to tackle each of the recommended actions, so that you can clearly understand the consequences of both action and inaction. The book doesn't tell you, screen by screen, *how* to implement any of the recommended **controls**; there are plenty of big, fat books out there that already do this, **operating system** by operating system (for example, Windows 95, 98, 2000, NT 4.0, Windows XP, Server 2003) and version by version. Because you only run one system, you only need a small bit of the information in each book. You don't need to be able to implement controls in a wide range of **systems**, as long as you can implement them in the one you actually run. This book gives you, in one set of covers, everything you need to know about the *what* and the *why*: enough for you to ensure that a trained IT person actually does what you need done.

STRUCTURE

All readers should read Chapters 1 (Threats and compliance) and Chapter 2 (Simply essential) and all business readers should also take in Chapter 9 (Legal and regulatory essentials); thereafter, readers should focus on the chapter (between 3 and 6) that most closely reflects their digital organizational set-up. Essentials for **wireless** networking (Chapter 7) and Essentials for **e-commerce** (Chapter 8) are both areas that might interest organizations of all sizes and the security issues are fairly common.

The alphabetic glossary section of the book is designed to underpin the content of the preceding chapters and can also be used as a direct reference tool. All those terms that appear in bold throughout the book are explained in the glossary. The glossary also highlights key controls (KC) and significant risks (SR) in order to make it easy to identify areas of concern.

This book does not provide guidance on the design and implementation of an **Information Security Management System** that might meet the specification of BS 7799/ISO 17799; an entirely adequate book (*IT Governance: A Manager's Guide to Data Security and BS 7799/ISO 17799*) already exists to do this. Readers are, therefore, referred to that book for detailed guidance on meeting the requirements of the standard. Readers, particularly from larger organizations, who are interested in the broader **IT governance** agenda are referred to *IT Governance: Guidelines for Directors*.

Acknowledgements

Some of the material in Chapter 1, and several of the definitions or explanations in the glossary, originally appeared in the 3rd edition of *IT Governance: A Manager's Guide to Data Security and BS 7799/ISO 17799*. I considered it important to maintain consistency between the two books and readers of both books will, hopefully, experience a sense of familiarity with this material.

Much of the content of Chapter 9 also originally appeared in *IT Governance: A Manager's Guide to Data Security and BS 7799/ISO 17799* and I would like to repeat here my thanks to Mark Turner, a partner in the IP/IT department of the London office of the international law firm, Herbert Smith, for his insightful comments on this material and for bringing to it the benefit of his many years experience advising companies in the IT and e-commerce sectors.

1

Threats and compliance

We live in an analogue world and, increasingly, work, play and do business in a digital one. Our assets, the things we own in either world and that are valuable to us, are also attractive to others. As we've extended our field of activity into the digital **world wide web** (or **internet**), as we've developed new technologies and acquired new skills, so we've been followed by all those antisocial elements who plagued us in the analogue one.

Over the centuries, we've become accustomed (particularly in the First World) to taking appropriate precautions around our analogue assets, health and security. We know how to secure homes, offices and cars. We know what precautions to take while walking, shopping or doing business. We know which neighbourhoods to stay out of. We teach our children what to do, and we have well-developed police and justice systems that deal (to one extent or another) with miscreants.

Although the police and justice systems are still coming to grips with the digital world, the miscreants – criminals (of all sorts: organized, white collar and occasional), malefactors, spies and other undesirables – have already successfully adapted their modus operandi to **cyberspace**. Of course, that doesn't mean that they've deserted the analogue world, they've just extended their sphere of operations to the digital one. We've therefore got to get as good at dealing with the cyber **threats** and **risks** as we already are at dealing with the analogue ones.

In the same way that the CEO of a business can understand the Profit and Loss statement without needing to be an accountant, or the average individual can understand the rules for maintaining and driving a motor car without having to be an auto-mechanic, so any business person or computer user can understand how to be safe online, without needing to be a computer expert. Just as you would be hard-pushed to help a medical specialist diagnose and cure an illness, without first having a good idea of what it takes to stay healthy, or what disease feels like, so it would be difficult to ensure that your business IT infrastructure, home network or personal computer was adequately secured – or even to call in appropriate outside help – without some grasp of the ABCs of information security.

THREATS

This book's purpose is to arm non-technical business executives and computer users everywhere with the basic information they need if they are to ensure that they and their businesses stay safe online. Staying safe online requires a combination of behaviour and tools that are appropriate and proportionate to the cyber-threats and computer-related risks that we face. Our starting point, therefore, must be to understand the threats and risks. A threat is 'potential cause of an unwanted **incident**, which may result in harm to a system or organization' and a risk is the 'combination of the probability of an event and its consequence' (both definitions from **ISO 17799:2005**). A threat and a risk are not, in other words, the same thing. There are many threats that pose no risk to individual organizations (for instance, the **hacker** threat poses no risk to someone who doesn't use a computer, and the grave **cyber-terrorism** threat poses a limited risk to a small organization whose only use of the internet is for e-mail). We will deal, here, with threats and, in the next chapter, with risks and **risk assessment**.

Threats in the digital world, as in the analogue one, originate with people. These people fall into five groups:

■ criminals (thieves, fraudsters, organized crime);
■ malefactors (hackers, vandals, terrorists, cyber-warriors, some ex-employees and other disgruntled or vengeful individuals);
■ spies (commercial and governmental);
■ undesirables (scam artists, spammers (see **spam**), 'ethical' hackers and nerds); and
■ the incompetent, or the simply unaware (staff, contractors, customers and other third parties).

From an organizational perspective, these people are found both inside and outside the organization (the balance overall is probably 50:50), but from a standalone computer perspective, there's only you.

Incompetence, lack of awareness and lack of skill are similar problems in either space. The digital threats, and the type of attacks that express them, have the same sort of objectives as they do in the analogue world, but because of the nature of computers, digital data and the internet, their characteristics are different. These characteristics, as identified by Bruce Schneier (2000), are:

- Automation: computers automate mundane tasks; illegal or destructive activity, with which someone would struggle to cost-effectively achieve critical mass in the analogue world, can be automated. Computers make **denial of service attacks** and large-scale junk mail possible, just as they enable 100 per cent surveillance of the internet communications traffic of any individual or organization.
- Data collection: digital data requires less storage space than the equivalent analogue information and can be more quickly harvested, stored and mined. What can be done will (often) be done and, as a result, massive databases of personal and commercial data now exist all over the world. They make spamming (see **spam**), surveillance and **identity theft** that much easier.
- Action at a distance: in cyberspace, the bad guys are just a mouse click away; the criminal who is trying to steal your money may be based in Chechnya, Moldavia or on a Pacific island. He or she will be just as effective, quick and silent as a criminal next door, far harder to trace and arrest than his or her analogue equivalent, and financially more successful.
- Propagation: the web enables ideas, skills and digital tools to be shared around the world within hours. It also enables techniques to be widely replicated and a vast array of computers to be linked into any one attack.

The types of attacks, therefore, that we have to be ready to deal with in cyberspace, are:

- criminal attacks (fraud, theft and grand larceny, identity theft, hacking, extortion, **phishing, intellectual property (IPR)** and copyright theft, piracy, brand theft, '**spoofing**');
- destructive attacks (cyber-terrorism, hackers, ex-employees, vengeful individuals, **cyber war**, cyber-vandals, anarchists, **viruses**);
- nerd attacks (denial of service attacks, publicity hounds, **adware**)
- espionage attacks (data and IPR theft, **spyware**).

These attacks affect individuals and businesses indiscriminately. Individuals and small businesses are rarely directly or individually targeted in an attack (unless they have very substantial assets or some other significant value to the attacker), but they are nevertheless at risk in an environment where automation, action at a distance and propagation enable an attacker to successfully target a very big number of smaller fish. Malefactors know that the majority of individuals and smaller businesses have inadequate cyber-protection and they exploit this, for instance, deploying large numbers of unprotected computers in huge **zombie** networks, to mount large-scale denial of service attacks and to distribute floods of **spam**. Defences need to be proportionate.

Large businesses and public sector organizations, who have significant assets to protect or who make attractive, high-profile targets, are directly threatened. Their networks are more extensive and more complex, and the quantity and diversity of people and organizations involved with them so great, that they have to be very systematic in identifying and responding to the possible threats.

Impacts of information security breaches

A 2001 global study by the UK DTI found that lapses in security **policy** had cost businesses between 5.7 per cent and 7 per cent of annual revenues in 2000. European businesses alone, it claimed, lost more than £4.3 billion in that year due to internet-related crime. Its seventh annual Information Security Breaches Survey (**ISBS** 2004), managed by Pricewaterhouse-Coopers (www.security-survey.gov.uk) identified the following symptoms:

One-third of large businesses and two-thirds of all companies still have no **information security policy**.

Processes for keeping **anti-virus software** up to date are often weak.

Only half of all wireless **networks** have security controls in place.

Spam is a growing issue (probably now 80 per cent of all e-mail).

Two-thirds of UK businesses had at least one malicious security breach in the last year, an increase from just under half two years earlier.

Over a quarter of businesses suffered a significant incident arising from accidental systems failure or data corruption.

The average UK business now has one security incident a month; large businesses have one per week.

Security breaches continue to cost UK industry several billions of pounds every year.

Organizations were significantly more pessimistic about the future outlook for information security breaches, believing that incidents will happen more often in future and be harder to detect.

The majority of businesses are still spending less that 1 per cent of their IT budget on security; the benchmark against which their expenditure should be compared is in the range of 5 to 10 per cent. Part of the problem may be that less than half of all businesses ever estimate the return on their information security investment.

The UK National High Tech Crime Unit's (www.nhtcu.org) 2004 survey produced the following key findings:

- Of all respondents, 167 out of 201 had experienced high tech crime in 2003.
- The total estimated impact of these crimes was over £195 million.
- Three out of 44 financial service companies experienced financial fraud of over £60 million between them.
- Almost three-quarters of respondents agreed that the single most important impact of a computer-enabled crime was whether the company could continue to operate, function and do business with its customers.

Ernst & Young (www.ey.com/global/content.nsf/International/Home) has been publishing an annual Information Security Survey since 1993. Its 2004 survey interviewed nearly 1,300 executives across 51 countries. Only 20 per cent of organizations strongly agreed that information security was a CEO-level priority, and only 24 per cent gave their information security departments the highest rating in meeting the needs of the organization. This suggests that there is a direct correlation between the effectiveness of the information security department and the informed, focused interest of the CEO. This handbook will help every CEO get better performance from that department. The executive summary of the EY survey made two observations:

> Since the release of our first survey in 1993, Ernst and Young has examined the various dimensions of information security as practiced by global organizations. Ironically, this year's survey seems to echo the sentiments of previous years, as organizations apparently continue to rely on luck rather than proven information security controls. Perhaps the remarkable thing is how little attitudes, practices and actions have changed since 1993 – during a period when threats have increased significantly. Two factors lead us to believe matters have deteriorated.

> First the threats are more lethal than they were in 1993. What many organizations are slow to recognize is that what they don't know is hurting them and hurting them badly. While scaremongers focus the public's attention upon the external threats with questionable damage guess-estimates, organizations face greater damage from insiders' misconduct, omissions, oversights, or an organizational culture that violates pre-existing policies and procedures.

Second, there is little visible change in how security is practised by organizations. In 1994, a respondent told us: 'It is apparently going to take a major breach of security before this organization gets its act together.' Some ten years later, that sentiment is still quite evident and typifies organizations' reluctance to deal with the significant threats and to invoke well-accepted controls.

The top five incidents identified in the Ernst & Young survey affected more than 50 per cent of organizations. Hardware failure that brought down critical business systems, the top incident, affected 72 per cent of the respondents. Does this mean that they now have tried and tested **business continuity plans** in place? Revealingly, less than 50 per cent of the respondents thought that they would be able to continue business operations in the event of a serious disruption.

Cybercrime

Europol, the European Police agency, observed in its 2003 report on EU organized crime: 'The establishment of worldwide financial markets, economic globalization, and the creation of the EU common market have provided good opportunities for organized crime groups.' In section 4.4, the report observes that 'organized crime groups are clearly among the major beneficiaries of technological progress. . . crucially, the development of cyberspace [has] provided great opportunities and a vast arena in which organized crime groups can operate. . . High technology crime will continue to represent one of the major areas of crime in the future, paralleling the development of e-commerce and internet banking.'

The US Computer Security Institute (CSI) has, with the participation of the San Francisco Federal Bureau of Investigation's Computer Intrusion Squad, conducted nine annual surveys into information security at CSI member firms. The results of the 2004 survey showed that 2004 total financial losses to criminal abuse, across the 269 respondents, were $141 million. While the biggest loss arose from viruses ($55 million) and denial of service attacks ($26 million), $11 million of these losses was from theft of proprietary information against $8 million for financial fraud and $7 million in laptop thefts. It was clear that the other half of those who took part in the overall survey were unable (because they had no method of tracking) or unwilling (because of the possible reputational damage) to provide estimates of the financial losses from the successful attacks they suffered. It is also clear that incidents of **cybercrime** originate equally from outside and inside the attacked computer systems.

Finally, the magazine *Information Security* carried out an online survey of 2,545 information security practitioners in a broad spectrum of public and private organizations in North America, Europe and the Far East. Although this was carried out in July and August 2001, its findings are still very relevant:

A virus, **worm**, **Trojan** or some other form of **malware** had affected 90 per cent of the organizations – even though 80 per cent of them had antivirus software in place.

The number of organizations hit by web server attacks doubled in number between 2000 and 2001.

Insider security incidents occurred more often than outsider ones, but security professionals were more concerned about securing the external **perimeter** of the organization than dealing with the internal issues.

These internal security incidents included installation of unauthorized software at 78 per cent of the participant organizations, use of company computing resources for illegal or illicit communications or activities (such as porn site surfing or e-mail harassment), and the use of company computing resources for personal profit (gambling, unsolicited e-mail or spam, personal e-commerce businesses, etc).

Many of these so-called information security incidents are actually crimes. The UK's **Computer Misuse Act 1990** made it an offence for anyone to **access** a computer without authorization, to modify the contents of a computer without authorization, or to facilitate (allow) such activity to take place. It identified sanctions for such activity, including fines and imprisonment. Other countries have taken similar action to identify and create offences that should enable law enforcement bodies to deal with computer misuse.

Cyber war

On 12 September 2001, the US General Accounting Office (GAO) reported that 24 US federal bodies, from the Treasury to the Pentagon, had computer systems 'riddled with weaknesses'. It recognized the ease with which hackers could read or tamper with critical information. On 18 September 2001, the Nimda worm infected and shut down 100,000 computers worldwide within 24 hours. It is believed that every significant terrorist or criminal organization has cyber-capabilities and has become very sophisticated in its ability to plan and execute attacks using the most recent technology.

Eliza Manningham-Butler, Director General of the UK's Security Service, said this at the 2004 CBI annual conference:

A narrow definition of corporate security including the threats of crime and fraud should be widened to include terrorism and the threat of electronic attack. In the same way that health and safety and compliance have become part of the business agenda, so should a broad understanding of security, and considering it should be an integral and permanent part of your planning and Statements of Internal Control; do not allow it to be left to specialists. Ask them to report to you what they are doing to identify and protect your key assets, including your people.

Certainly, businesses have got this message, with 97 per cent of them concerned at board level about cyber-terrorism. They should be. More than 400 million computers are linked to the internet; many of them are vulnerable to indiscriminate cyber-attack. The critical infrastructure of the First World is subject to the threat of cyber assaults, ranging from defacing websites to undermining critical national computer systems. In February 2003, the White House published the National Strategy to Secure Cyberspace, in which the President recognized that securing cyberspace 'would be an extraordinarily difficult task, requiring the combined and coordinated effort of the whole of society and that, without such an effort, an infrastructure that is essential to our economy, security and way of life could be disrupted to the extent that society would be debilitated'.

Future risks

There are a number of trends that lie behind these increases in threats to information security, which, when taken together, suggest that things will continue to get worse, not better:

▓ The use of distributed computing is increasing. Computing power has migrated from centralized mainframe computers and data processing centres to a distributed network of desktop, laptop and micro-computers, and this makes information security much more difficult.

▓ There is a strong trend towards mobile computing. The use of laptop computers, **Personal Digital Assistants (PDAs)**, mobile phones, digital cameras, portable projectors and MP3 players has made working from home or on the road relatively straightforward, with the result that **network perimeters** have become increasingly porous. There are many more **remote access** points to networks, and the number of easily accessible **endpoint devices** has increased dramatically, increasing the opportunities to break into networks and steal or corrupt information.

▓ There has been a dramatic growth in the use of the internet for business communication, and the development of wireless, **VoIP** and **broadband** technologies will drive this even further. The internet provides an effective, immediate and powerful method for organizations to communicate on all sorts of issues. This exposes all these organizations to the security risks that go with connection to the internet:

- Better hacker tools are available every day, on hacker websites that, themselves, proliferate. These tools are improved regularly and, increasingly technologically proficient criminals – and computer literate terrorists – are thus enabled to cause more and more damage to target networks and systems.
- Increasingly, hackers, **virus writers** and spam operators are co-operating to find ways of spreading more spam: not just because it's fun, but because direct e-mail marketing of dodgy products is lucrative. Phishing and other internet fraud activity will continue evolving and will become an ever bigger problem. This will lead, inevitably, to an increase in **blended threats** that can only be countered with a combination of technologies and processes.
- Increasingly sophisticated technology defences, particularly around user authorization and **authentication**, will drive an increase in **social engineering**-derived hacker attacks.
- Widespread computer literacy. While most people today have computer skills, the next generation is growing up with a level of familiarity with computers that will enable them to develop and deploy an entirely new range of threats. **Instant messaging** is an example of a new technology that is better than e-mail, because it is faster and more immediate, but which has many more security **vulnerabilities** than e-mail. We will see many more such technologies emerging.
- Wireless technology – whether **WiFi** or **Bluetooth** – makes information and the internet available cheaply and easily from virtually anywhere, thereby potentially reducing the perceived value and importance of information and, certainly, exposing confidential and sensitive information more and more to casual access.
- The falling price of computers has brought computing within most people's reach. The result is that most people now have enough computer experience to pose a threat to an organization, if they are prepared to apply themselves just a little to take advantage of the opportunities identified above.

What does this all mean, in real terms, to individuals and to individual organizations?

- No organization is immune.
- Every organization, at some time, will suffer one or more of the abuses or attacks identified in these pages.

∎ Individual and business activity will be disrupted. Downtime in business critical systems (such as ERP [enterprise resource planning] systems) can be catastrophic for an organization. However quickly service is restored, there will be an unwanted and unnecessary cost in doing so. At other times, lost data may have to be painstakingly reconstructed and, sometimes, it will be lost forever.

∎ **Privacy** will be violated. Organizations have to protect the personal information of employees and customers. If this privacy is violated, there may – under **data protection** and privacy **legislation** – be legal action and penalties, including against directors individually.

∎ Organizations and individuals will suffer direct financial loss. Protection in particular of commercial information and customers' **credit card** details is essential. Loss or theft of commercial information, ranging from business plans and customer contracts, to intellectual property and product designs, and industrial know-how, can all cause long-term financial damage to the victim organization. Computer fraud, conducted by staff with or without third-party involvement, has an immediate direct financial impact.

∎ Reputations will be damaged. Organizations that are unable to protect the privacy of information about staff and customers, and which consequently attract penalties and fines, will find their corporate credibility and business relationships severely damaged and their expensively developed brand and brand image dented.

The statistics are compelling. The threats are evident. No one can afford to ignore the need for information security. The fact that the threats are so widespread and the sources of danger so diverse means that it is insufficient simply to implement an anti-virus policy, or a business continuity policy, or any other standalone solution. A conclusion of the CBI Cybercrime Survey 2001 was that 'deployment of technologies such as firewalls may provide false levels of comfort unless organizations have performed a formal risk analysis and configured firewalls and security mechanisms to reflect their overall risk strategy'. Nothing has changed.

COMPLIANCE, REGULATORY AND LEGAL ISSUES

Certainly, organizations can legally no longer ignore the issue. There are a number of pieces of UK legislation that are relevant to information security: the **Copyright Designs and Patents Act 1988**; the **Computer Misuse Act 1990**; the **Data Protection Act 1998**; the **Human Rights Act 1998**; the **Electronic Communications Act 2000**; the **Freedom of Information Act 2000**; **Regulation of Investigatory Powers Act 2000**; the **Privacy**

and Electronic Communications Regulations 2003 and the Software Licensing Regulations.

Apart from the Freedom of Information Act (which came fully into force in January 2005), the Data Protection Act (**DPA**) 1998 is perhaps the most high profile of these recently passed laws; it requires organizations to implement data security measures to prevent unauthorized or unlawful processing (which includes storing) and accidental loss or damage to data pertaining to living individuals. Non-computerized or manual records, videotape and microfilm, are all also covered by this legislation. According to BSI, the UK Information Commissioner has stated that organizations that can demonstrate compliance to BS 7799 will be able to satisfy his office that appropriate measures are in place to meet the security requirements of the DPA.

While these Acts apply to all UK-based organizations, stock exchange listed companies are also expected to comply with the recommendations of the Combined Code on Corporate Governance and the Turnbull Guidance. Crucially, these require directors to take a risk assessment-based approach to their management of the business and to consider all aspects of the business in doing so.

The implications of this are that directors of listed businesses and of public sector organizations must be able to identify the steps they have taken to protect the **availability**, **confidentiality** and **integrity** of the organization's information assets. In all of these instances, the existence of a risk-based information security management policy, implemented through an Information Security Management System (ISMS), is clear evidence that the organization has taken the necessary and appropriate steps.

INFORMATION SECURITY

So, what is 'information security'? 'Information security' is, according to the internationally recognized code of information security best practice, ISO 17799:2005, the 'preservation of the confidentiality, integrity and availability of **information**; in addition, other properties, such as authenticity, **accountability**, **non-repudiation** and **reliability** can also be involved'.

Information is the life blood of the modern business. All organizations possess **critical** or sensitive information. According to a 2000 UK Department of Trade and Industry survey, 49 per cent of organizations believe that information is critical or sensitive because it will be of benefit to competitors, while 49 per cent believe that it is critical to maintaining customer confidence. The 2004 survey identified the fact that, while 58 per cent of all businesses had highly confidential information stored on their computer systems, 77 per cent of large businesses were in this category.

Roughly nine-tenths of UK businesses now send e-mail across the internet, browse the web and have a website; and 87 per cent of them now identify themselves as 'highly dependent' on electronic information and the systems that process it, compared with 76 per cent in 2002. Information and information systems are, in other words, at the heart of any organization trying to operate in the high-speed wired world of the 21st century.

The proliferation of increasingly complex, sophisticated and global threats to this information and its systems, in combination with the compliance requirements of a flood of computer- and privacy-related regulation around the world, is forcing organizations to take a more joined-up view of information security. Hardware-, software- and vendor-driven solutions to individual information security challenges no longer cut the mustard. On their own, in fact, they are dangerously inadequate.

News headlines about hackers, viruses and online fraud are just the public tip of the data insecurity iceberg. Business losses through computer failure, or major interruption to their data and operating systems, or the theft or loss of intellectual property or key business data, are more significant and more expensive.

This handbook provides business owners, executives, general managers and individual users in organizations of all sizes and types with an overview of the information security needs of their organization. It enables them to understand what their IT management is telling them, to sort the wheat from the chaff, the jargon and the hype from the real issues and to make pragmatic information security decisions that are right for their business, rather than just right for the IT people. This handbook provides sufficient information and insight to help the reader navigate the dangerous sea of technology-specific solutions pitched by vendors and/or the IT department. It does this by looking at the actual threats facing organizations of different sizes and types, recognizing that there are no 'one size fits all' solutions, but that there are some basic principles (the **Infosec Basics for Business**) that should underpin all responses.

Organizations that want to take a more structured approach to information security (developing, for instance, an Information Security Management System) and to their overall strategy for managing information and their information assets should be looking to develop an IT governance framework. They are referred to two books, both complementary to this one, that will help them achieve this: *IT Governance: Guidelines for Directors* and *IT Governance: A Manager's Guide to Data Security and BS 7799/ISO 17799*.

BENEFITS OF TAKING ACTION

▮ Individuals will decrease the likelihood of suffering disruption, inconvenience and from the effects of cybercrime.

▮ Directors of listed companies will be able to demonstrate that they are complying with the requirements of the Turnbull Guidance and/or complying with current international best practice in **risk management** with regards to information assets and security.

▮ Organizations will be able to demonstrate, in the context of the array of relevant legislation, that they have taken appropriate action to comply with the laws, particularly (in the United Kingdom) the Data Protection Act 1998.

▮ Organizations and individuals will have systematically protected themselves from the dangers and potential costs of external or internal attack, cybercrime and the impacts of cyber war.

▮ Each organization will improve its credibility with staff, customers and partner organizations and this can have direct financial benefits through, for instance, improved sales.

▮ Better, informed, practical decisions about what security technologies and solutions to deploy will reduce the overall costs of information security while improving the effectiveness of those investments.

▮ Directors will be able to ensure that the information security solutions that are deployed help the business progress, rather than hinder it – that the technology becomes a 'business enabler', leading to improved performance.

The major benefit, overall, is that the **logical** world will become more like the analogue one to which we have become used over the last few centuries: safe, predictable and prosperous.

2

Simply essential

OVERVIEW

Organizations of all sizes, big and small, have to take action to deal with information security (infosec) threats. That action should be appropriate and proportionate to the risk and your **risk appetite**. You don't have to be secure against everything, you don't have to buy every bit of security hardware or software that is forced on you and, yes, it may be true that some infosec firms have overstated the size of a threat as well as the benefit of their solution.

A core information security concept is that, for each clearly identifiable risk, there should be an equally clearly identifiable control – if, that is, a decision has been made to accept the risk. Another key concept is that, before you can decide whether or not to accept the risk, you need to assess what the risk actually is, which means you need to identify the likelihood of the threat and its possible **impact**.

There are, however, a number of controls that are so basic that every business of any size needs to implement them. These are contained in the **SOHO Internet Highway Code** and the Infosec Basics for Business. These controls, which relate to the most widespread, frequent and pervasive information security threats, are so basic that they are at the heart of the international code of best practice in information security, ISO 17799:2005. You don't need a risk assessment or to bring in an information security specialist to tell you to take action. If you think it's sensible to lock your office when you go home, to lock your car when you leave it in the street and keep your wallet zipped safely away, then you should be following the SOHO Internet Highway Code in a small office/home office and ensuring the Infosec Basics for Business are implemented in a larger one.

SOHO Internet Highway Code

The SOHO Internet Highway Code provides guidance for the secure management of a standalone computer or a micro-network in a small office or home office. It has 10 essential principles:

1. Safeguard your computer.
2. Use a strong password and a **screensaver**.
3. **Update** and patch your operating system.
4. Have an up-to-date **firewall**.
5. Have up-to-date anti-virus software.
6. Act anti-spam.
7. Use up-to-date **anti-spyware**/adware tools.
8. Be sensible – don't take unnecessary risks.
9. Back it up.
10. Fix problems as soon as they arise.

Of course, there is a lot of detail in each of these principles, which are discussed in Chapter 3, but any business that applies all 10 will be secure from the vast majority of threats that might be encountered.

Infosec Basics for Business

The larger business environment is different from that of a small business in two ways: firstly, the majority of people using computers in the business do not actually own the computers, and so are unlikely to have an owner's interest in their security; and, secondly, the more complex the organization, the more likely it is to handle a greater range of business and information demands, to have a more complex computer infrastructure, to have exposure to a wider range of threats and to have more at risk.

There are, however, 14 basic information security principles that all organizations need to implement: the Infosec Basics for Business. They contain an organizational perspective on the essentials that are in the SOHO Internet Highway Code, and are designed to operate alongside that code. In other words, the Infosec Basics provide basic guidance on the minimum security standards that should be implemented in organizations of any size, and the Internet Highway Code can provide guidance for their employees on their role in the implementation of that strategy. Every organization should issue all their employees – and particularly employees who are **teleworkers** or **mobile workers** – with a copy of the Internet Highway Code alongside an organization-specific **user agreement**.

While the basics should be implemented in every business, they are only a starting point, not a final solution. A final solution will be the result of moving beyond the basics. All businesses should, once the basics are satisfactorily in place, assess the entire spectrum of threats and risks they face and implement controls that will deal adequately with them. Risk assessment is covered later in this chapter.

The Infosec Basics for Business are:

1. Have a policy.
2. Insist on accountability and responsibility.
3. Identify asset ownership and **classification**.
4. Address information security in contracts: all employment and **third party** contracts must include information security.
5. Provide for the **physical security** of information systems.
6. Have up-to-date **anti-malware software**.
7. Implement and enforce user **access controls**.
8. Implement and enforce **system access controls**.
9. Manage **vulnerabilities**.
10. Have an incident response process.
11. Have basic **business continuity** and **disaster recovery plans**.
12. Monitor **compliance**.
13. Document the essential policies, **processes** and procedures.
14. Ensure that users are trained and aware of their responsibilities.

RISKS AND CONTROLS

The linked concepts of risks and controls are fundamental to Information Security Management Systems. Risk is defined as 'the combination of the probability of an event and its consequences'. Control is defined as the 'means of managing risk, including policies, **procedures, guidelines**, practices or organizational structures, which can be of administrative, technical, management or legal nature; [the word is] also used as a synonym for safeguard or countermeasure'. (Both definitions are from ISO 17799:2005.) You should only deploy controls that relate to, and are appropriate and in proportion to, the actual risks you face. ISO 17799:2005 contains a list of all the best-practice controls that might be considered in relation to the whole range of risks, and BS 7799 provides a specification for an Information Security Management System that reflects deployment of this best practice. A BS 7799 system is probably not appropriate for a small organization, but should certainly be considered by larger SMEs and should be a prerequisite for large organizations.

In larger organizations, there needs to be a **risk treatment plan** based on a risk assessment and the corporate risk appetite; in smaller organizations, the Infosec Basics need to be implemented with the same sort of conscientiousness normally applied to car maintenance, or to wearing a seatbelt. It may also – depending on the risks – be necessary for a smaller organization to do more than just the basics.

RISK ASSESSMENT, IMPACT AND RISK MANAGEMENT

All organizations face risks of one sort or another on a daily basis. Risk management is a discipline for dealing with non-speculative risks, those risks from which only a loss can occur. Speculative risks, those from which either a profit or a loss can occur, are the subject of the organization's business strategy, whereas non-speculative risks, which can reduce the value of the assets with which the organization undertakes its speculative activity, are (usually) the subject of a risk management plan. These are sometimes called permanent and 'pure' risks, in order to differentiate them from the crisis and speculative types. Usually, the identification of a risk as either speculative or permanent reflects the organization's risk appetite.

Risk management plans generally have four, linked, objectives. These are to:

1. eliminate risks;
2. reduce those that can't be eliminated to 'acceptable' levels; and then to either
3. live with them, exercising carefully the controls that keep them 'acceptable'; or
4. transfer them, by means of **insurance**, to some other organization.

Pure, permanent risks are usually identifiable in economic terms; they have a financially measurable potential impact upon the assets of the organization. Risk management strategies are usually therefore based on an assessment of the economic benefits that the organization can derive from an investment in a particular control; in other words, for every control that the organization might implement, the calculation would be that the cost of implementation should be outweighed, preferably significantly, by the economic benefits that derive from, or economic losses that are avoided as a result of, its implementation. The organization should define its criteria for accepting risks (for example, it might say that it will accept any risk whose economic impact is less than the cost of controlling it) and for controlling risks (for example, it might say that any risk that has both a high likelihood and a high impact must be controlled to an identified level, or threshold).

This chapter is intended only to provide an introduction to and overview of risk management. There is more detailed guidance on this process in *IT Governance: A Manager's Guide to Data Security and BS 7799/ISO 17799* (Chapter 6). Appropriate training should be sought by anyone who is going to perform this activity on a regular basis. A systematic approach to risk assessment should take into account business, legal and regulatory requirements placed on the business. In other words, it must be business-driven. This is one of the most important ideas in information security: the business, managed by its board of directors, should identify the threats to assets, vulnerabilities and impacts on the organization and should determine the degree of risk that it is prepared to accept – in the light of its business model, business strategy and investment criteria. Risk assessment is a 'systematic study of assets, threats, vulnerabilities and impacts to assess the probability and consequences of risks' (ISO 17799: 2005) or, in our terms, the systematic and methodical consideration of: 1) the business harm likely to result from a range of business failures; and 2) the realistic likelihood of such failures occurring.

The risk assessment should be a formal process. In other words, the process should be planned and the input data, its analysis and the results should all be recorded. 'Formal' does not mean that technical risk assessment tools must be used although, in more complex situations, they may improve the process and add significant value. The complexity of the risk assessment will depend on the complexity of the organization and of the risks under review. The techniques employed to carry it out should be consistent with this complexity and the level of assurance required by the board.

Who conducts the risk assessment?

Unless the organization already has a risk management function, staffed by people with training that enables them to carry out risk assessments, it will (depending on the complexity of the organization) need to delegate the responsibility to someone. There are two ways of doing this. The first is to hire an external consultant (or firm of consultants) to do it. The second is to train someone internally. The second is preferable in most cases, as the risk assessment will need to be reviewed when circumstances change and having the expertise in-house enables this to be done cost-effectively. If the organization already has a trained information security adviser, this person should take on the role.

In circumstances where the organization has existing arrangements with external suppliers for risk assessment services, or is in the process of setting up a risk management function or capability (in the context of responding to the requirements of the Turnbull Guidance, perhaps), then it should from the outset ensure that its information security risk assessment process is included.

It is more difficult for a smaller business to retain specialist information security expertise in-house than for a larger one; the internal risk assessment role needs to be maintained over time and the person concerned needs to continue being trained and involved in risk assessment issues, both inside and outside the organization. The disadvantage of hiring external risk assessors, apart from the level of cost, is that the organization does not necessarily get adequate continuity. The advantage of the external hire, apart from it being a variable cost, is that the external assessor should be up to date on relevant issues and should be wholly objective. A possible middle route is to contract on a multi-year basis, with an appropriately trained individual or consultancy firm to personally provide this service as and when it is required.

Risk analysis

Qualitative **risk analysis** is by far the most widely used approach (and is the approach expected by BS 7799). Risk analysis is a subjective exercise in any environment where returns are derived from taking risks – and it is preferable to be 'approximately correct, rather than precisely wrong'. All individual inputs into the analysis will reflect individual prejudice, and so the process of information gathering should question inputs to establish what really is known – and what is unknown. The process is as follows:

▨ Identify and document in tabular form (in what will become the organizational **risk log**) all the information assets in the organization and which individual and/or department 'owns' the asset. It is worth ranking the systems in terms of their criticality to the organization; those systems on which the organization is most dependent for its business survival will be those that should have information security priority. The least important ones can be addressed later.

▨ Identify all the threats for each identified asset. A threat is something that can go wrong or that can 'attack' an asset. They can be either external or internal. Examples might include fire or fraud; many such potential threats are described in Chapter 1. Threats are always present for every system or asset – because it is valuable to its owner, it will be valuable to someone else. For each of the assets, threats should be considered under the headings of confidentiality, integrity and availability. Some threats will fall under one heading only, others under more than one. Assume that, if you can't identify a threat to an asset, it is not really an asset.

■ Identify all the potential vulnerabilities each asset has for each threat. Vulnerabilities leave a system open to attack by a threat or allow an attack to have some success or greater impact. For example, for the external threat of 'fire', a vulnerability could be the presence of inflammable materials (for example, paper) in the server room. A vulnerability can be exploited by a threat.

■ Identify the possible impacts that the successful exploitation of a vulnerability by a threat will have on the asset's availability, confidentiality or integrity (**impact analysis**). These impacts should all, wherever possible, be assigned an estimated monetary value, using a category system (for example, less than £1k, between £1k and £10k, etc) that reflects the size of the organization and the total cost (direct and indirect) of the incident.

■ Assess the probability of the event occurring, using a **classification system** such as once every few years, once per year, once every six months, etc. **Virus** attacks would fall into the every day category.

■ This then enables one to identify the level of risk (and, pragmatically, a low–medium–high classification is usually adequate) and then to conclude, for each risk, whether it is acceptable or if some form of control is required.

Controls

These are the countermeasures for risks. Apart from knowingly accepting risks that fall within the criteria of acceptability, or transferring the risk (through insurance) to others, there are four types of control:

1. Deterrent controls reduce the likelihood of a deliberate attack.
2. Preventative controls protect vulnerabilities and make an attack unsuccessful or reduce its impact.
3. Corrective controls reduce the effect of an attack.
4. Detective controls discover attacks and trigger preventative or corrective controls.

It is essential that any controls implemented are cost-effective. The principle is that the cost of implementing and maintaining a control should be no greater than the likely cost of the impact. It is not possible to provide total security against every single risk; there is a trade-off that amounts to providing effective security against most risks.

Risk management

All organizations, once they have implemented the Infosec Basics, should at least consider carrying out a more formal risk assessment. Larger organizations will certainly need to, as the Infosec Basics will be inadequate for the wide range of risks that they face. No organization, though, should invest in information security technology (hardware or software) or implement processes and procedures, outside of the Infosec Basics, without having carried out an appropriate risk assessment that assures them:

▪ that the proposed investment (the total cost of the control) is the same as or less than the cost of the identified **event**'s impact;
▪ of the **risk classification**, which takes into account its probability; and
▪ of the priority of the risk – that is, have all the risks with higher prioritizations been adequately controlled?

If the organization cannot satisfy itself that the proposed investment meets these criteria, it will be wasting money – and the time required to implement the control – while leaving itself open to more likely risks and, conceivably, with inadequate resources to respond to the more likely risk when it occurs. There is, in other words, a risk associated with not doing – and maintaining – an adequate risk assessment and directors should carefully consider this risk (and their fiduciary duties) before proceeding without one.

3

The SOHO Internet Highway Code

Anyone running a small business network (up to 10 computers) in a small office or a home office (SOHO) is part of a key target market for today's online crime gangs. The reasons are simple: people operating standalone computers and micro-business networks usually have neither the expertise nor the resources to effectively secure their networks. This means that cyber criminals are easily able to commandeer these networks and deploy them as zombies, component parts of the **botnets** they use for carrying out **distributed denial of service (DDoS)** attacks or for spam distribution. Computers in micro-networks are even more likely to be infected by viruses, spyware, Trojans and worms, more likely to be the victim of automated hacking **exploits** and more likely to be the means by which these attacks are multiplied.

In addition, micro-businesses are even more dependent on their computers and their networks than larger ones; typically, they are less resilient, less able to survive business interruptions of any size, and more dependent on critical information and intellectual capital.

For these businesses – the owners or managers of which usually have other interests than technology – a clear set of basic security principles is essential. Such a set of basic principles is contained in the SOHO Internet Highway Code.

THE 10 RULES OF THE SOHO INTERNET HIGHWAY CODE

1. Safeguard your computer.
2. Use strong passwords and a screensaver.

3. Update and patch your operating system.
4. Have an up-to-date firewall.
5. Have up-to-date anti-virus software.
6. Act anti-spam.
7. Use up-to-date anti-spyware/adware tools.
8. Be sensible – don't take unnecessary risks.
9. Back it up.
10. Fix problems as soon as they arise.

IMPLEMENTATION GUIDANCE

The implementation guidance below for each of these rules is aimed at people with a single computer installed in a small office or home office, and at people who, if they are operating two or more computers, are doing so either on a **peer-to-peer** network or on a small network with a single internet **gateway**. You should apply all these rules to each user and computer on the network. In other words, the guidance focuses on single computers but assumes that, in multiple computer situations, you will apply it to each computer. And you will need to do this – your security is only as strong as your weakest link, and if one user (perhaps someone who only uses a computer once per week) switches off anti-virus protection or leaves a password in clear text on a website, you may never recover!

If you are operating a small office business network, you should also read about *security in contracts* in Chapter 4, the Infosec Basics for Business, and consider applying that guidance in your relationship with your colleagues. You might also, for completeness, review the rest of the Infosec Basics for Business (in Chapter 4) to identify whether or not there are any other specific additional steps that you could profitably take.

Identify your operating system

The first step is for you to identify your operating system. If your computer is a Macintosh, go to www.apple.com/support/security/ for further advice. If it is a Windows PC, then you need to identify which version of Windows you are running. Go either to *Control Panel – System Properties – General*, which will show you the Windows version you are running, together with details of the latest **service pack** you have installed, or to http://www.microsoft.com/athome/security/protect/default.aspx and click on *Find out which version of Windows your computer is using*. The website will check your computer and tell you what version of the Windows operating system is installed. The **configuration** steps in this guide relate to Windows XP but the principles apply to all Windows operating systems, and the implementation steps (identified here in *italics*) for older operating systems are usually similar to those identified here. If you are not running Windows XP, arrange to upgrade as soon as possible; the security structure of XP is *so much better* than anything that came before it. If you have more than one operating system running within a small office/home network, consider standardizing on the most advanced: it will make life much simpler for you.

Before you even go online:

1. Safeguard your computer

a) Workstations should be set up in a secure, clean, calm, stable environment. You don't want them exposed to animals, dirt, machinery, chaos or anything else that might damage any part of the machine. You don't want them balanced on a pile of books or boxes from which they might topple.

b) Don't have (large coils of) loose cables that might be a safety hazard; tripping over a cable and pulling it out of the computer – or pulling the computer over – might not be something you want to do.

c) Always log out of and shut down Windows, and switch your computer off when it's not in use. Don't switch your computer off without having first logged out; you may damage some programs.

d) Install an **Uninterruptible Power Source (UPS)**. While household power supplies are in theory protected from power surges, they are not immune from power failure. Your UPS will save you losing your work if there is a failure. You can buy them inexpensively from computer shops and they should be designed to:
   i. deal with any mains power surges that might harm your computer;
   ii. continue running for long enough, in the event of a power cut, for you to log out of and shut down your computer in an orderly way.

e) Ensure that your physical internet connection (switch or **modem** cable) is easily accessible and clearly marked, so that you can disconnect it urgently should you need to. Make sure that it won't get easily or mistakenly disconnected by someone else. 'Always on, always vulnerable' so, if you have a broadband connection and you're not using the internet but leaving your computer switched on, disconnect; this will make it impossible for someone to access your machine while you're away from it.

f) Laptops need special care and attention. The rules about using them in a safe place are even more important, because laptops are only too often balanced precariously or used in the midst of all sorts of other activity:

i. More laptops are stolen or lost while travelling than from the home. When travelling, try to make your laptop bag look inconspicuous; more importantly, when you're not using it, keep it under your feet (under the airplane seat in front of you, for instance) or on your lap. Assume that someone nearby would love to steal it.

ii. Keep a close eye on it when you go through a security checkpoint – someone might grab it while you're distracted by something or someone else. Don't leave it behind on the checkpoint conveyor belt because you're in a hurry. Be paranoid.

iii. Watch for snoops looking over your shoulder to see your financial data before they steal the laptop.

iv. Make sure that your computer(s) are all appropriately covered under your business insurance policy.

v. Think about how you will handle **backups** while you're travelling.

g) Pay equal care and attention to the security of your **PDA** and mobile telephones. While they're not as valuable as your laptop, someone will want to steal them and you're not going to enjoy dealing with this loss in a foreign country.

2. Use strong passwords and a screensaver

a) You probably log into your computer as '**administrator**'. This is the most powerful class of user that can operate your computer; an administrator can change anything, delete anything, hide anything, steal anything, corrupt anything and use your computer to do anything, legal or illegal – and you'll never be able to prove it wasn't you who did it. So it's not too clever to make it even vaguely easy for just anyone passing by to log into your computer and wield this sort of power.

b) If your computer is a standalone, and kept in a relatively private area, then you should go to *User Accounts* in *Control Panel* and:

i. Use *Change an account* to change the **user name** from 'administrator' to your own preferred user name (how about a variant of your own name?), because this at least doesn't look quite as interesting to a potential miscreant.

ii. Require the use of a password – make it something that is not easy for a miscreant to guess – so don't use consecutive letters, numbers, your birthday (or anyone else's), a family member or your dog's name, or anything equally obvious (so 'password' would be a bad choice). Don't choose a word from the dictionary (hackers use automated **dictionary attacks**). Use something that is at least seven characters long. Make it a mix of upper case and lower case, and mix numbers, letters and symbols. This will make it difficult for someone to guess. Don't write your password on a post-it note – or anything else – that you keep anywhere near the computer. If you think someone might have guessed it, change it (in *Change an account*). The simplest way to create a password that you can remember is to create a phrase (for example, 'hackers should be taken out and shot') and to use the first letters of each word as the password (for example, 'hsbtoas'), then build in a numeral, a change of case and a symbol (for example, 'hsBtoas7$'), which probably gives you something pretty uncrackable.

iii. It is particularly important that any password you use over the web (that is, for accessing your bank account) is a strong one.

iv. By all means, use the same password for a number of sites and services – it's difficult to remember more than one or two strong passwords – but see the advice in 6 h), below, about disposable e-mail addresses for use on the internet.

v. And, be sure to change your password, on all those websites, every three to four months – just in case someone somewhere has intercepted a communication containing it but doesn't yet have the rest of the information necessary to do damage to you.

vi. Unless you first contacted them (and you're sure you really got through to them) NEVER give your password to someone who asks you for it, irrespective of the reason they offer or the apparent genuineness of their credentials (including their website). If someone asks you for your password, they're up to no good. Don't give it to them. Not even if they tell you that you'll be banned from the internet forever and have all your money frozen.

c) If your computer is part of a small network, or kept in a busy area, or is accessible by a number of other users, or is operated by someone in your team, particularly computer-savvy ones, you need to be more careful. Go to *User Accounts* in *Control Panel* and:

i. Carry out the steps identified in 2 b) above for the administrator user name, but make the password really hard to guess. You're not going to use this account again, except for administrator-type functions, so file the password somewhere very safe – and nowhere near your computer.

ii. Select the *Guest Account* and *turn it off*. This will stop anyone who doesn't even have a user name using this group account to access your computer without your permission.

iii. *Create a new account*, using a variant of your own name for the user name, make it a *Limited account*, and make it password-protected, following the guidance of 2 b) ii. above. This is the account that, in future, you should use for all your computer activity.

    iv. If someone else is going to use your computer, create a separate user account for that person, following the guidance above. Whenever you are going to change computer user, have one user log out as a user before the other user logs in.

d) Set up a password-protected screensaver in *Display Properties* (in *Control Panel*); choose a delay before the screensaver operates (10 minutes is probably practical) and tick the *On resume, password protect* box. You can even choose what the screensaver looks like. You can now be sure that, if you walk away from your machine without logging off, it will automatically protect itself from access by a miscreant taking advantage of the fact that you are already logged in. When you return, you type in your password (the one you set pursuant to 2 b) ii. above) and you're back in business.

3. *Update and patch your operating system*

a) One reason why there are so many viruses and hackers out there is that **Microsoft**'s Windows product is so vulnerable and is so widely distributed. It's got lots of faults – the consequence of ever more complex code, with ever more sophisticated features, rushed out as fast as possible. Some people recommend installing some other operating system – anything but Microsoft. The argument in favour of installing some **browser** other than **Internet Explorer** (such as **Firefox**) and some e-mail package other than **Outlook** or **Outlook Express** (such as **Eudora** or **Thunderbird**) is even stronger. We don't think it's necessary, but you really have to make your own decisions, particularly about browser and e-mail. We do think that, if you are running a small network, you should standardize on one **application**. We think that Microsoft has all the features, pretty well everyone else is using their software and, after all, you already know how to use it – you just want to do so securely. That means patching the holes and updating the software as often as you can.

b) Microsoft release **hot fixes**, **patches** and **upgrades** to their software as and when vulnerabilities are identified and they've adequately tested the new code. Hot fixes are released as soon as possible, once a significant vulnerability is identified; patches are released on a standard monthly cycle, and **service packs** are released about once per year. Service packs make improvements as well as consolidating previous patches and hot fixes, but that is not a reason to delay updating until the upgrade arrives, because you probably won't survive uninfected and unhacked for that long.

c) Log your computer on to http://www.microsoft.com and go to Windows Update in the left hand menu. This will take you to a page that can automatically scan your computer to see what **updates** are required; ask it to identify which high priority updates are required. It will produce a list of the available updates. Follow the on-screen instructions to **download** and install them. It would be sensible to ensure, before you start any downloads, that your telephone access will not be interrupted until you have finished the download and you might need to consider, if you don't have a broadband or ISDN connection, having Microsoft mail very big updates (service packs, for instance) to you on a CD ROM – or you may be online for an expensive few hours while the download runs its course.

d) Once you know that your computer is running a fully updated version of the operating system, keep it that way. Windows XP (also Windows 2000 with SP3 and Windows ME) all support **automatic updates**, a feature that automatically checks for the availability of updates whenever you are online and downloads them to your computer for you to install. You do have to configure this feature – in *System Properties*, where you want to tick the setting that downloads updates automatically, doesn't install them but alerts you (with a balloon at the bottom of your screen) so that you can. This does give you the option, if you have an urgent task to complete immediately after logging on, to do so before you commence installation; automatic update might significantly affect your ability to carry out any other task in parallel.

e) Keep yourself informed: Microsoft provides an e-mail update service that provides non-technical alerts for users about security issues and software updates. Register for the newsletter on: http://www. microsoft.com/athome/security/default.mspx.

f) You should also update and patch your applications; if you are running Microsoft Office, go to the Office (http://office.microsoft.com) page, click *Downloads* and arrange to have any identified updates installed. These are less important than Windows updates and patches.

4.   Have an up-to-date firewall

a) A firewall is essential for any computer – and needs to be either on the network gateway, or on the computer – and, in certain situations, on both.

b) Of course, you can't think why anyone should attack your machine – but it's the automated hacks (see **automated hacking scripts**) that will do the damage – who wants their computer to be a part-time member of a massive zombie network used for distributed denial of service attacks, spam distribution or illegal data storing? You're in slightly less danger if you use a dial-up connection than if you have (permanently on) broadband; this is because, although your **IP (Internet Protocol) address** is permanent if you are on broadband and changes every time you log on with dial-up, the whole global range of IP addresses can be scanned and checked by an automated hack or worm every 15 minutes. You probably also don't want to risk someone else being able to see any of your financial transactions or to access any of your private data – like bank records.

c) If you are operating a small network with a single internet gateway, you will need to install a firewall on the gateway. If you can afford it, also install a **router** that has a built-in firewall between your computer modem and your computer or network.

d) You need to install a personal firewall on standalone computers, on each computer in a peer-to-peer network and also on each computer in a SOHO network. Installing a firewall is not rocket science. Microsoft XP (SP1 and SP2) provides a default firewall, which is better than nothing. Even Microsoft doesn't pretend that their firewall is a replacement for good third-party products. There are a number of firewalls, some free, others not. There are a number of criteria to consider in choosing a firewall (including integration with anti-virus software, protection for instant messaging, etc). Don't think 'free' is a long-term solution.

e) You need to have updated your anti-virus protection, and run an anti-virus system scan before you download your firewall.

f) BEFORE you download a third-party firewall, you need to turn off the Microsoft XP default firewall. Two firewalls DO NOT equal twice as much protection: they equal a false sense of security and NO PROTECTION! Go to *Control Panel – Windows Firewall* and tick the *Off, not recommended* button. Don't hang around now; go get the third-party product you've already chosen.

g) If you are running on a broadband connection, you need to test your firewall; services are available that will carry out inexpensive **penetration testing** and you should test your firewall immediately after installation and on a monthly basis (or after any significant software changes) thereafter.

h) You also need to keep your firewall up to date; your firewall software and supplier should have an automatic update feature that will alert you to needed updates and download them for you as and when they become available.

i) You should familiarize yourself with the basics of your firewall, rather as you familiarize yourself with the basics of car maintenance or home security. You will have a few new things to do, including allowing both incoming and outgoing internet activity (because, for instance, if your firewall alerts you to all outgoing activity, it's sure to detect a Trojan phoning home), and there may be minimal set-up decisions to make when you install the product. Follow the online 'help' instructions provided with it (usually the default option is adequate) or, if necessary, contact the provider's helpdesk.

5. Have up-to-date anti-virus software

a) There are some 100,000 viruses, worms and Trojans circulating in the wild. Some of them are worse than others, and some very nasty indeed. You must install anti-virus software, both to protect your computer from infection and to stop your computer infecting others.

b) Your **ISP** should have anti-virus software installed at its internet gateway, and this should catch the majority of virus traffic. It is not foolproof and you don't want to rely on it alone.

c) You need to install anti-virus software on standalone computers and on each computer in a peer-to-peer network. You need to have anti-virus software even if you only use webmail. Don't bother trying to find free stuff; anything that's any good costs money to keep up to date, so get used to it. Anti-virus software has to do many things, not the least of which is catching and eliminating today's new viruses, worms and blended threats. It also has to integrate with your firewall and spam **filter**, find viruses that might have come in via instant messaging, on a CD ROM or on a **USB stick**, or on an e-mail downloaded from a webmail account. This means that you probably want an integrated anti-virus and firewall product. Anti-virus software must come from a reputable supplier and must be the latest version of their software.

d) You should run only one anti-virus package; two or more will conflict and also slow your machine down. If you are changing anti-virus suppliers, uninstall your current package (*Control Panel – Add or Remove Programs*) before installing the new one.

e) Once you have chosen, and installed, an anti-virus software package, familiarize yourself with it, in much the same way as you familiarize yourself with how to maintain (oil, water, petrol, etc) your motor car. Ensure that the software is up to date and is set to automatically update itself (preferably) daily. Weekly is no good. New viruses appear every day. Weekly updates are like closing the stable door after the horse has left the country. Daily is just about enough.

f) Run a complete system scan (following the instructions that come in your product's control panel); this may take about an hour, but you want to be sure that any known viruses currently on your system are identified and quarantined before you go any further.

g) Your vendor probably produces a virus-warning and update news-letter; register for it and pay attention to its advice. Some viruses propagate around the world before the anti-virus companies have produced a defence against them, and you want to find out that there's a problem before it's too late. If you find the idea of a different regular newsletter from each vendor (Microsoft, firewall, anti-virus, anti-spyware, etc) unexciting, register for an infosecurity warning service, which encapsulates all the security information from all the key Internet Highway Code security areas (and covering all the technologies, including **cellphones**) that you might need – or want – to have.

h) DON'T fall for **virus hoaxes** – these are usually in the form of an e-mail telling you to watch out for a particular virus and recommending that you pass the e-mail on to everyone you know. Don't. If it is a virus, it will already have been described in that newsletter service from your vendor; you don't want to be guilty of forwarding a whole load of spam, do you?

i) DON'T open e-mail attachments (including .txt ones, and especially not anything with a .exe, .scr or .pif extension) from people you don't know or which you don't specifically recall asking to have sent to you. Be particularly careful of 'zipped' files. DON'T open files sent to you in instant messaging, unless you know the sender and really, really need to open their file. Chances are, it'll contain a virus that your anti-virus software won't have the opportunity to detect until after it's downloaded to your computer.

6. Act anti-spam

a) Spam is e-mail that you don't want, that clogs your inbox, trying to sell you all sorts of things that you don't want. It is bulk e-mail, sent by someone you don't know, and it may be commercial, political, religious, fraudulent or simply malicious in nature. You don't want to read it. You really don't. There's a lot of it about: some estimates are that 80 per cent of all e-mail is now spam.

b) There is also bulk e-mail that you DO want to receive and, because you want to receive it, it isn't spam. A spam filter is software that tries to sort the spam from the ham: to identify and block the incoming spam but to let through what you want to receive.

c) Major ISPs (AOL, Yahoo, MSN, BT Openworld, etc) all provide gate-way spam filters but, of course, they won't always correctly identify individual messages: some that shouldn't get through will, and others that should reach you, won't. If yours is a corporate machine, a spam filter should already be installed on your corporate e-mail gateway.

d) You want to ensure that any e-mail that does reach your computer is sorted, with the stuff you want going into your inbox and the stuff you don't want going into your junk mail box. This means that you need to have spam filtering software on your computer as well as whatever exists for the ISP and it requires that you set specific rules for your spam filter, so that it knows what you want to have excluded.

e) The major ISPs provide inbox-level spam filters as well as the gateway ones and, if you use one of these ISPs, you should use this facility to set the level of filter that you require. You may need to use trial and error until you get something that works for you.

f) Outlook 2003 has an inbuilt junk mail filter. You set it by going to the Outlook toolbar, choosing *Tools – Options – Preferences – Junk E-mail* and then choosing the level of protection that you prefer. You should probably not have stuff automatically deleted, as the filter may filter out e-mails you actually want to see. You should check the junk mail folder from time to time, identify e-mails that have been incorrectly filtered, add the sender to your *Safe Senders list*, by right-clicking on the e-mail and, from the drop-down menu, choosing *Junk E-mail – Add Sender to Safe Senders list* (or you could choose any of the other options available).

g) A number of anti-virus packages come with spam filters. You should be wary of running more than one spam filter on your computer at a time, because the complication of getting two sets of filter rules configured correctly is probably not worth the effort. If you're running Outlook 2003, you're probably adequately protected, so disable any other filters. There's no need, though, to worry about the two conflicting and providing no filtration between them.

h) Make sure that spammers can't get your e-mail address:

    i. DON'T let anyone get your real e-mail address. If you're going to leave an e-mail address on lots of websites, in chat groups and chat rooms, then get a disposable e-mail address (for example, from hotmail – perhaps a different one for each activity) and then replace it every now and then. Whatever happens, don't leave your real e-mail address available for a spammer's spambot to find.

    ii. DON'T leave ticked those boxes that say it's OK for a vendor and all its partners to send you information.

    iii. DON'T ever respond to **spam** – if you do, even to say 'Go Away', it proves you exist and may be gullible and so will raise you up the target list. Don't try to unsubscribe from a spam e-mail – it also has the effect of proving your existence and possible naivety. It's simpler to set your spam filter to block the sender completely (**'blacklisting'**).

iv. DON'T ever open spam; unless you know and trust the sender, assume that any junk e-mail message may also have a **payload**, such as a virus or a piece of spyware or adware – or that opening it may just send a message to the sender that you exist and are possibly gullible.

v. DON'T let your e-mail address list in Outlook get out of date; remove people you don't want to correspond with but do add those you want to hear from. It helps your filter know what it should let through ('**whitelisting**').

vi. Another option is to use 'disposable' e-mail addresses. See www.spamhelp.org/services/listings/verification for information about providers of this service. It can be time consuming, though.

7. Use up-to-date anti-spyware/adware tools

a) Spyware and adware are different from viruses and hackers. Adware is **pop-up** advertising software that has downloaded to, and runs on, your computer, usually without your active consent or knowledge. It will try to keep a series of advertisement windows open in front of you, irrespective of your attempts to close them. You may have agreed to the installation (by clicking the '*I Agree*' declaration when downloading, for instance, a peer-to-peer tool such as Kazaa) and sometimes it is contained within some **shareware**, **freeware** or other plug-in (for instance, an animated cursor) you downloaded, or was triggered by an advert you clicked. Spyware is software you didn't deliberately install, which collects information about you (for instance, by logging your keystrokes when you type passwords) and sends it across the internet to some third party – who might then use the information to defraud you or simply to send you targeted advertisements ('trackware').

b) Both adware and spyware consume substantial amounts of **CPU** power, slow your machine down, bombard you with pop-ups that get in your way, alter websites you visit, sometimes crash your computer and generally make your life a bore – as well as bringing an increasing torrent of spam to your inbox. You really want to keep adware and spyware to a minimum.

c) Keep away from the more unsavoury websites and follow the advice in 6 f) iii. and iv. above.

d) The first step is to clean up your machine. Download the Microsoft anti-spyware program from www.microsoft.com/downloads, install and run it. The installation process takes about 15 minutes, but if you just follow the instructions it can be completed painlessly. Configure it for automatic updates, and for real time protection. Once it is installed, have it run a complete disk scan and then follow the advice it gives you about any adware or spyware it detects. For preference, unless you have a good reason for retaining anything it detects (a good reason might be that a shareware/freeware program you genuinely want to retain requires you to live with the adware), remove it.

e) If you are unable to clean up your computer (that is, in spite of installing all updates, running anti-spyware and a virus scan, your machine is still not working properly), you may have a more serious problem. Go to 9 below for initial advice.

f) Once you have a clean machine, avoid further infestation:

    i. Don't download shareware, freeware or other plug-ins unless you really know and trust the company that produced them and you have some evidence that they don't come with a payload. Read the EULA (End User **Licence** Agreement) and any other documentation that exists to establish the integrity of the supplier – see our advice in 8, below.

    ii. Don't install a **dialler**, even if it says it's for free – it probably isn't. The expense may be much more than you bargained for. In any case, you are already connected to the internet. If you can only get to that site by downloading their dialler, just forget it!

    iii. Don't close any window or website by pressing a button that says '*Agree*' or '*OK*' as this may also download something to your computer – ALWAYS click the red 'x' in the top right-hand corner of the window to close it.

    iv. Don't allow just any website to install **cookies** on your computer: in Internet Explorer, choose *Tools – Internet Options – Privacy* then set the slider to at least *Medium*; if you're particularly paranoid, set it to *High* and see how well that works for you. Note that the default setting for Windows XP SP2 is *Medium*.

    v. Don't click on links in Instant Messenger or in **chat rooms**, unless you know and trust the person who sent it to you, and you really, really need to follow the link – it might take you to a (spoofed) website that installs adware, spyware or something even nastier.

    vi. If you really, really do want to go to a site for which someone has sent you a link, and you are a bit suspicious of it, then type the **URL** into the browser window, rather than clicking the link – it is possible to spoof a link.

g) Keep anti-spyware up to date (set it for automatic updates), and be sure to run a system scan on a regular basis: at least once per month.

8. Be sensible – don't take unnecessary risks

a) Be alert – pay attention – be sensible. As we said at the beginning, the bad guys are just a mouse click away from you. You'll be fine, as long as you take sensible precautions.

b) Ensure that you follow the Internet Highway Code – and it's the first seven rules that are particularly important!

c) When you're surfing the web, pay attention: if a website asks you for personal information of any sort, be very careful about providing it; if you're offered a cool piece of software, be very wary about downloading it; when you do want to buy something, be sure that your vendor is genuine and likely to deliver what you think you're buying.

d) Assume that, if you're on a questionable site, the chances of something going wrong are much greater: for instance, you're much less likely to tell your spouse, friends and children about having your credit card details ripped off if you were on a porn site than if you were on Amazon.com.

e) Good sites can sometimes also give you problems: if someone has hijacked the site and is using it to take advantage of a current flaw in your software, you may be caught.

f) If something starts going wrong while you're on the internet, or on a website, hit the STOP button. Your firewall should have such a button, so find it and know how to use it. If you want even faster disconnection, pull out the cable that connects you to the internet. Once you're safe, figure out what happened, fix it and install whatever future protection you need to avoid a repeat (see 9, below), and only once you're clean and safe should you venture back onto the internet.

g) Another basic rule of life also applies: 'If it looks as though it's too good to be true, it probably is'. Everything has a price, even if you can't see it right now – the real price might be the theft of your identity, followed by all your money.

File sharing

a) Peer-to-peer networks provide opportunities for files on your computer to be shared by other users. You might be happy with this; on the other hand, you might be concerned about someone else being able to change, delete, add to or corrupt data in the files on your computer, or about the fact that **file sharing** is a straightforward way for viruses to spread.

b) Disable file sharing: *Start – Settings – Network Connections – LAN or High Speed Internet*; then right click on each icon and, in the *Connection Properties* dialogue box, unclick *File and **Printer** Sharing*.

c)   If you are using a file sharing system to try to get round copyright law for online music sharing and purchases, you want to hope that you don't get hurt.

Identity theft

a)   This is a relatively straightforward crime: if someone can establish themselves as you, they could borrow a large amount of money (that you would then have to repay), spend all the money you've actually got, and perhaps even sell your assets for you – your house, for instance. Before you worry about the house, you should worry about the debts and credit card bills that will ruin your credit rating forever – because, even once you've proved that it wasn't really you who incurred them, chances are they will still be sitting on your credit file.

b)   What does someone need in order to pretend they're you? Well, your name, address, date of birth and some proof of identity – usually a combination of credit card and utility bills. And where's the best place to get all of this? The documentary stuff comes from your rubbish bin (particularly easy if you send the discarded stuff off for recycling) and the date of birth from an online cv, from an online genealogical/ family tree activity, or from some form of social engineering attack ('You may have won a huge prize, if you were born on the right day! What's your date of birth? Oh dear, that's not the one we're looking for.' It is.)

c)   There are some very simple rules:
   i.   Buy a shredder (less that £70 from almost any stationery shop) and USE it – after all, that's what the people who send you those documents say you should do with them!
   ii. Don't put your date of birth in an online cv at a recruitment site (in these officially non-ageist days, it shouldn't be necessary any-way).
   iii. Don't put your date of birth into any 'family history' online search.
   iv. Don't fall for any of the social engineering attacks. Nothing is for free – especially not money.
   v.   Keep a close eye on what happens to any official documentation – driver's licence, passport – if anyone's desire to look at it seems unusual (particularly abroad – remember that foreigners are usu-ally seen as easy prey, because they don't really know what's going on and they're going home shortly anyway) – assume it is – this is just another form of a social engineering attack.

Internet cafes and other public computers:

a) Public computers could have **keystroke loggers** or other spyware that have been physically installed; someone could snoop and, when you leave the computer, someone else could find out where on the internet you've been. Any or all of these possibilities risk your bank account being cleared out, your credit card details stolen, or your files and other information accessed.

b) So, be sensible. When you're using a public computer (particularly abroad):

    i.   Don't save login information: log out of websites by pressing *'Logout'* rather than closing the window, and disable any 'automatic login' options.

    ii. Don't enter sensitive information (for example, credit card details, passwords in full) onto public computers, unless you're entering them into **Secure Sockets Layer (SSL)** sites.

    iii. Watch out for snoops (people reading over your shoulder) and don't leave the computer unattended (to get a coffee, for instance) with sensitive or confidential information on the screen – log out, or have a (real) friend stand guard.

    iv. On completion, erase your tracks. In Internet Explorer, click *Tools – Internet Options – General*, then *Temporary Internet Files – Delete Cookies* and then *Delete Files*, then *History – Clear History*.

Online auctions

a) Research the auction site: ensure that it is genuine, reputable, that its dispute resolution policies are robust and look for guarantees that you will be refunded if you have been scammed. Don't be attracted offsite to do a deal with someone who can offer you 'something better for a direct trade' – this person will almost certainly scam you.

b) Research the seller: ensure that there is a telephone number (that works) rather than just a PO Box, and look for evidence that the seller has done business before – in the form of online feedback.

c) Research the item: is it likely to be genuine or, if it appears to be very cheap, is it likely to be a copy, imitation, fake or stolen item? Remember, if it's too good to be true, it probably is.

d) Research the proposed delivery method and timetable: if it's not going to be shipped virtually immediately, assume the vendor wants some time to disappear with your money.

e) Research the proposed payment method: use an **online payment service**, follow the guidance about payment options below, and question any changes in payment address made after completion of the bidding.

f) Never respond to phishing requests to update your personal details.

Online payment services

a) Online payment services can all be used to pay safely for goods and services – although you should always be wary of a phishing site posing as one of these.
b) Remember that, if you use your credit card to fund your PayPal account, your card company is likely to treat that single transaction as the only one it has liability for, so that any later payments out of your PayPal account that are disputed will have to be resolved with PayPal directly. The basic rule is, always, to expose as little money at a time as you have to.

Online recruitment services

a) These are an ideal hunting ground for identity thieves. You should:
   i.   Be prudent in how many sites you put your cv on.
   ii. Limit the information you provide: for instance, don't include your date of birth, age or home address, and consider using a temporary e-mail address that you use only for cvs.

Online shopping

a) Safest methods of payment are, in order from best to worst, credit card – and then there's a big gap, followed by: debit card, digital wallet, cheque and, worst of all, cash. This is because you can at least dispute a transaction on your credit card statement before it is due for payment whereas, if you have already parted with the money, it is somewhat harder to get it back. Credit card companies also offer liability limitation policies for fraudulent purchases – you need to know what your own card company's policy is.
b) Online stores are usually, but not always, legitimate; certainly, the more mainstream the product, the more likely they are to be above board. You should be careful about doing business for the first time with any online store – you don't want to provide your personal and credit card details to a fraudster.
c) Check the 'Contact Us' pages. You want to find a street address and a telephone number that you can call and arrange for a catalogue or something to be sent to you that proves the firm really exists. You also want to be doing business with a company that is based in a jurisdiction whose laws you respect and under which you might be able to take action, so compare the country shown as being the physical address of the organization with the jurisdictional details

contained in the Terms of Business posted on the website. No Terms of Business? No business.

d) You also want to find a 'privacy policy' on the site. Read it: are you happy with the arrangements the website is making to protect your privacy?

e) The danger really comes when you enter your details to purchase something. If payment is taken through an online payment service, you're relatively safe. If the online store is taking your details directly, you want to be sure that you are entering information into a secure site (look for a change in the URL to one that begins **https** (there should also be a small locked padlock in the bottom right-hand bar of your browser), and make sure that you don't provide anything more than is essential – your mother's maiden name, for instance, might not be essential.

f) Look for a 'trustworthy website' certificate. A number of organizations offer this type of certificate; their standards and usefulness vary, so the basic rule is to click on the certificate, or otherwise trace it back to the issuing authority, and satisfy yourself as to the validity and value of the certificate before using the website.

PDAs and mobile phones

a) Viruses now exist for mobile phones and PDAs. Bluetooth enables a third party to access your mobile telephone numbers. Both PDAs and mobile phones carry lots of data that, if lost, could inconvenience or hurt you.

b) Think about passwords and keyboard locks for both.

c) Keep an eye on developments (that infosecurity alert newsletter), so that you can take appropriate action in relation to viruses and other threats.

d) Read Chapter 7, which deals with **wireless networking**, cellphone and PDA security issues in considerable depth.

Phishing

a) Phishing is an online scam designed to get personal information, such as credit card details, bank account numbers, passwords, etc – online identity theft. The miscreant sends out spam, providing a link to what looks very much like a genuine website (but is in fact a spoofed one), asking you to provide updated personal details.

b) The most important rule is: never respond to these e-mails. No reputable organization will ever send you an e-mail asking you to update your personal information. None – not ever. If you are in doubt, phone the institution (get their telephone number from some source other than the data included in the e-mail).

c) If you think you won't be able to resist going to one of these sites, even though you know that your financial institution will NEVER, not UNDER ANY CIRCUMSTANCES ask you to visit a site and input key details like your user name and password, then at least get yourself a 'truth bar' – an internet browser bar that will tell you where the website you are visiting is actually located, how long ago it was set up, etc – this will at least enable you to worry about why your apparently reputable London bank only set its website up yesterday in a Middle Eastern country. If, after this, you still choose to give them your critical personal details, please expect to lose all your money.

d) Before entering any confidential information into a website, check that it is a secure site: the web address should start with https and there should be a locked padlock in the bottom right-hand corner of the browser. Double-click this icon to see the security certificate and confirm that the name on the certificate matches that of the business whose site you think you're visiting.

e) Check your credit card and other statements. Investigate anomalies immediately. Report suspected abuses to your financial institution, to the police and, if possible, to the company whose website may have been spoofed.

Scams, frauds, 419s

a) These do happen on the internet. Read the advice contained elsewhere in rule 8 of the Internet Highway Code to remain safe and secure.

b) A 419 (or Nigerian Advance Fee) scam is one that offers to make you millions of pounds richer is you would just help out a poor bureaucrat somewhere with your bank account details, or a small sum of money, so that they can get things moving. If it's too good to be true, it probably is.

Spoofed e-mail addresses and websites

a) Spoofing is making a transmission look like it came from someone else, or a website look like a reputable one.

b) E-mail 'returned to sender' with an attachment – and which you don't recall sending – might be spoofed, with a virus. Don't open the attachment.

c). A web link sent to you (in spam, or by someone you don't know) might be to a spoofed site, which downloads bad stuff onto your computer or gives you an opportunity to give away all your critical information (phishing). Don't click the link. If you must go there, type the URL into your web browser – and then check the site out very carefully, particularly if it claims to be a financial services site.

Wireless networking

a) This is a particularly important area. Chapter 7 deals with the key wireless networking issues.

9. Back it up

a) The worst thing that can happen to you is that you lose everything on your computer. This could be because of a major system **crash**, a major malware **intrusion**, or some other disaster. You need to have copies of everything available so that you can recover yourself.

b) What's on your computer is, essentially, stored in two sorts of folder: program folders and information folders. CD ROM copies of everything in the program folders should have been supplied when you purchased the computer and you want to keep those, and the system documentation, in a safe place.

c) You should keep a paper list of any shareware/freeware or other programs (for instance, firewall, anti-virus, etc) that you have installed, together with website and purchase details, so that you can re-install them when you need to.

d) If you don't have important information stored in computer documents, you don't need to back it up. If you do have important information on your computer, you have to make backup copies of the relevant folders. The best way to do this is (for each user) to make a copy of either the whole *My Documents* folder or just those folders that you care about (for instance, you may not want to backup the *My Pictures* folder), on either a (one or more) floppy disc or CD ROM.

e) You should regularly update this backup; the safest way is usually to operate with two sets of backups, one that you made (say) a week ago, and one that you made today. You can re-use the oldest set of discs when you make today's backup. On any day that you make significant or important changes to your documents, make a backup.

f) If your information is particularly critical, you should arrange to keep these backups offsite – so that, if there is a fire or some other natural disaster, your critical information will survive it.

g) Online, browser-accessible backup services are now available that should be able to automate and make your backup easier – if you do a lot of work and need to make daily backups, these are probably the way to go.

10. *Fix problems as soon as they arise*

a) From time to time, something may get past your defences. It might be a virus, worm or Trojan. It might be a hack attack. It might be spyware. Whatever, your computer is not behaving as it used to. Sort the problem out as soon as possible – otherwise it is likely to get worse.

b) Tackle the possible issues step-by-step:

  i.   The first step is to disconnect your computer from your home network.

  ii. The next step is to have your anti-virus software run a complete system and disc scan. Close all your programs and run the scan. Wait for, and act on, the results of that scan.

  ii. The scan may identify that you have malware on your system that has bypassed your protective controls. Your anti-virus software might not be able to remove this code, so run the Microsoft Malicious Software removal tool – available from Microsoft downloads. It automatically downloads as a monthly security update and runs on your computer, detecting and eliminating any resident (active) malicious software. You might not want to wait for the next monthly update, so download it manually, and let it run and try to detect if you have active malicious code on your computer. Alternatively, if your scan identifies the virus, it might direct you to download a specific removal tool from its website. Do this. If this doesn't solve your problem, go to the next step.

  iv. The next step is to carry out an anti-spyware scan. Have anti-spyware carry out a full system scan. Wait for, and act on, the results of that scan – which should include removing any adware or spyware on your computer unless you are absolutely certain that you need it. If this doesn't solve your problem, go to the next step.

  v.   The next step is to carry out a broader security audit. The best way to do this is to go to http://www.securityspace.com/sspace/index.html and run their Free Trial Audit. This will tell you if you have vulnerabilities that a hacker might have exploited and is likely to point to openings in your firewall. This may lead you to increase the security setting of your firewall. Once you have done this, check to see if your computer is behaving properly. If not, there is one final step you can make before you call for outside help.

  vi. This final step is to restore your system to its configuration prior to the problem. *System Restore* will reverse ALL changes to Windows between today and any earlier date you choose, but won't change any data files. It will reverse everything, including updates and patches, so you don't want to have to go too far back – which is why you want to identify and deal with problems as soon as possible. *Start – Programs – Accessories – System Tools – System Restore* gets you to the place you want to be. Choose *Restore my computer to an earlier time*, then *Next*, then pick the date immediately before the day on which you think your problem occurred. Click *Next* until you're told to restart your system, and then restart it. Hopefully, your problem has now gone.

vii.   You can reverse the *System Restore* process, simply by going through the steps set out above and picking the most current date as the restoration date.

viii.   If, after doing this, you still have a problem, you should seek professional help.

4

The Infosec Basics for Business

INTRODUCTION

Information security in business is now too important to be left to the IT department. Information security is, in fact, now a boardroom issue, and this chapter deals with it from a management perspective. It provides guidance on an appropriate boardroom response to the information insecurity challenge and is relevant in organizations of all sizes.

Why is information security a boardroom issue?

- Information is the life blood of today's business. Anything that is of value inside the organization will be of value to someone outside it. The board is responsible for ensuring that critical information, and the technology that houses and processes it, are secure.
- Legislation and regulation are governance issues. In the United Kingdom, the Turnbull Guidance clearly identifies the need for boards to control risk to information and information systems. Data protection, privacy, computer misuse and other regulations – different in different jurisdictions – are a boardroom issue. Banks and financial sector organizations are subject to the requirements of the Bank of International Settlements (BIS) and the **Basel 2** framework, which includes information and IT risk.
- As the intellectual capital value of 'information economy' organizations increases, their commercial viability and profitability – as well as their share value – increasingly depend on the availability, confidentiality and integrity of their information and information assets.
- The scale of, and speed of change in, the 'information economy' is every day creating new, global threats and vulnerabilities for all networked organizations.

Threats and consequences

The one area today in which businesses of all sizes enjoy a level playing field is in information security: ALL businesses are subject to world-class threats, all of them are potentially betrayed by world-class software vulnerabilities and all of them are subject to an increasingly complex set of (sometimes contradictory) computer- and privacy-related regulation around the world.

While most organizations believe that their information systems are secure, the brutal reality is that they are not. Individual hardware-, software- and vendor-driven solutions are not information security systems. Not only is it extremely dangerous for an organization to operate in today's world without a systematic, strategic approach to information security, such organizations have become threats to their more responsible brethren.

The extent and value of electronic data are continuing to grow exponentially. The exposure of businesses and individuals to its misappropriation (particularly in electronic format) or destruction is growing equally quickly.

The growth in computer- and information-related compliance and regulatory requirements reflects the threats associated with digital data. Directors have clear compliance responsibilities, which cannot be met by saying: 'The CIO – or Head of IT – was supposed to have dealt with that', or 'I'm not really interested in computers and technology, the CFO deals with all that', or 'I'm more interested in the business strategy, really'.

Ultimately, consumer confidence in dealing across the web depends on how secure they believe their personal data is. Data security, for this reason, matters to any business with any form of web strategy (and any business without a web strategy is unlikely to be around in the long term). It matters, too, to any organization that depends on computers for its day-to-day existence (to produce accounts, for instance) or that may be subject (as are all organizations) to the provisions of the Data Protection Act. The Freedom of Information Act, which ostensibly applies only to public sector organizations, raises confidentiality issues for any business that contracts with the public sector, and requires the public sector to have systems that are capable of classifying and supplying the information requested.

Newspapers and business magazines are full of stories about hackers, viruses and online fraud. These are just the public tip of the data insecurity iceberg. Little tends to be heard about businesses that suffer profit fluctuations through computer failure, or businesses that fail to survive a major interruption to their data and operating systems. Even less is heard about organizations whose core operations are compromised by the theft or loss of key business data; they usually just disappear quietly.

Information security management today

Information security management, in the vast majority of organizations, is inadequate, unsystematic or, in practical terms, simply non-existent. That's partly because many boards still think of it as **computer security** and that it's therefore simply an ancillary responsibility of the people who run the computers. It's also partly because many boards have never really thought through the information needs (and therefore the information strategy) of their businesses. Either approach is Neanderthal and will quite properly lead to extinction. We live and work in the Information Age, where information is one of our most valuable assets and where, therefore, intelligent action to safeguard it is as necessary as safeguarding movable physical assets used to be in the Viking and Golden Horde eras.

Information insecurity also exists because organizations don't actually have the knowledge, resources or expertise to tackle it effectively. As a result, small and medium-sized businesses tend to be inaccurate in allocating (sometimes inadequate) resources (manpower, management time and hard cash) to deal with the most important, strategic, business security issues, while tackling individual threats and risks in a haphazard way. Investing in isolated solutions to individual threats leaves so many holes that it's only slightly more useful than not bothering in the first place. Some of the particular issues facing smaller organizations, and ways of dealing with them, are addressed in Chapter 5.

Larger organizations tend to operate their security functions in vertically segregated silos with little or no coordination. This structural weakness means that most organizations have significant vulnerabilities that can be exploited deliberately or which simply open them up to disaster. For instance, while the corporate lawyers will tackle all the legal issues (non-disclosure agreements, patents, contracts, etc) they will have little involvement with the information security issues faced on the organizational perimeter, or the way in which cyber law, cybersecurity and e-commerce have to interact for the real benefit of the customer.

On the organizational perimeter, those dealing with physical security concentrate almost exclusively on physical assets, such as gates and doors, security guards and burglar alarms. They have little appreciation of, or impact upon, the 'cyber' perimeter.

The IT Managers responsible for the 'cyber' perimeter may be good at ensuring that everyone has a password, and that there is internet connectivity, that the organization is able to respond to virus threats, and that key partners, customers and suppliers are able to deal electronically with the organization, but they almost universally lack the training, experience or exposure to adequately address the strategic threats to the information assets of the organization as a whole.

There are even organizations where the IT Managers set and implement security policy on the basis of their own risk assessment, past experiences and interests, with little regard for real needs or strategic objectives. What else could they do? They are not equipped to deal with the strategic, business information issues. Of course, users within the business recognize that these sorts of rules interfere with *doing business,* so the rules tend to be ignored – leaving the board with a false sense of assurance about the level of protection they enjoy. The specific issues of larger organizations, in both the public and private sectors, are touched on in Chapter 6.

The board's responsibility

The board's real responsibility is to create, in the context of its business model and strategic goals, an information strategy. Our concern in this book is, however, with information security. Information security is a complex issue. It deals with the availability, confidentiality and integrity of information assets – the valuable data sitting within business critical systems, and subject to world-class threats.

The range, scale and complexity of the threats, both internal and ex-ternal, and the increasing difficulty of legal and regulatory compliance, means that boards cannot afford to have loopholes in their information security systems. Therefore, one has to think in terms of securing the whole enterprise, the entire organization, which includes all the possible combin-ations of physical and cyber **assets**, all the possible combinations of intra-nets, **extranets** and internet interfaces, and which might include an extended network of business partners, vendors, customers and others. One has to look at the distribution and supply channels. One has to take into account the present and future information needs of the business, and the tech-nology required – today and tomorrow – for supporting them.

Inevitably, it's about the business model. It's about the strategic risks facing the business. And that means it's the board's responsibility. Yes, the board probably will need outside help to address the issues and, no, the board doesn't have to become expert in the technological minutiae of how information security is managed. But the board does have to face up to its information security responsibility.

Information Security Management Systems

An Information Security Management System (or ISMS) is the practical outcome of the type of approach recommended above. Smaller companies are unlikely to call it that, but it is still an ISMS. At heart, an ISMS is no more than a set of controls that reduces those risks the organization has decided to 'accept but control' to a level consistent with its **control standard**; and the framework within which those controls are operated. The Infosec Basics are, for instance, an ISMS, although not one designed to be capable of BS 7799 **certification**.

'Controls' are a blend of technological, procedural and behavioural components that, between them, achieve a specific identified and documented **control objective**. For instance, your desktop user systems are threatened by a malicious mix of viruses, worms, Trojans, **scumware** and spam, whose outcome will be to compromise the availability, confidentiality and integrity of the data on your desktop. The attack **vectors** are: e-mail, web surfing and instant messaging. The controls would include:

- technological – anti-virus and anti-spyware software, anti-spam filters, firewalls and automatic updating;
- procedural – configuration of the software and firewall, updating procedures, **incident management** procedures and **acceptable use policies**;
- behavioural – user awareness of and **awareness training** in dealing with these threats and methods of response, including recognizing when scumware is attempting to download onto a PC.

This three-way blend is typical of all effective controls; implementation of only two of them leaves a significant exposure that can undo everything that has been put in place. The false sense of security that most organizations derive from only having a partial solution in place can be particularly destructive.

Best practice

In this fast-changing and complex world, it is difficult for any one individual to identify all the threats that exist and the full range of possible, workable controls that might be deployed to counter them. There is no need to. Global best practice in information security has been harnessed and expressed in two documents that are fast becoming the cornerstone of organizational information security: BS 7799 and ISO 17799.

BS 7799:2005 (also known as ISO 27001:2005) is a sector-neutral specification for a vendor- and product-neutral ISMS and it contains, in Annex A, a comprehensive list of controls. It is a business orientated and risk assessment-driven standard that, whether or not an organization seeks external certification, is external proof of the quality of the organization's information security systems.

BS 7799 is supported by, and makes extensive reference to, the international code of practice, ISO 17799:2005. Whereas BS 7799 specifies what is required for an ISMS, ISO 17799 sets out, in substantial detail, what best practice considerations might be for each of the recommended controls.

These two standards, available from www.itgovernance.co.uk, can be combined with a detailed, practical handbook on how to achieve certification (such as *IT Governance: A Manager's Guide to Data Security and BS 7799/ISO 17799*) and a range of commercially available tools (document toolkits, risk assessment tool, also all available from www.itgovernance. co.uk) to ensure that best practice is being systematically deployed inside the business.

This book is not designed to help organizations achieve BS 7799 certification. Its advice is, though, derived from and compatible with the requirements of ISO 17799, the international Code of Practice, and any organization that wants to upgrade its ISMS from one developed following this book's basic advice will find the upgrade path relatively painless.

And all organizations should consider that upgrade path: in the information economy, where information control and exchange drives business success, a demonstrably secure information system becomes a significant business asset. The best way of demonstrating information security is for the ISMS to be subject to ongoing third-party audits that entitle the organization to a BS 7799 certificate.

THE 14 INFOSEC BASICS FOR BUSINESS

Every organization must implement, at the very minimum, a number of basic information security practices: the Infosec Basics. If you had the luxury of time (clue: you don't) and the threats were mostly in the future (clue two: they're not), you could afford to take the classical, formal approach to implementing information security: start with a risk assessment, develop a risk treatment plan, identify all the assets, assess the risks to them, determine the controls to be applied, etc. In practical terms, you've got to take a different approach; you've got to be sure you've implemented all the Infosec Basics first and then, only once you've got a basic level of security in place, you can revert to the classic approach: carry out the risk assessment, etc.

Yes, this does mean that the Infosec Basics will meet only the most basic security requirements of any business, and it does mean that (particularly larger) businesses will need to go a substantial way beyond them if they are to be adequately secure. In other words, information security controls must be implemented to differing levels (depending on the scale, complexity and nature of the risks that have been identified) in different businesses,. But the Infosec Basics are the starting point and (almost) any organization today that hasn't implemented the Infosec Basics is a danger to itself and a threat to all its more responsible corporate brethren.

Every organization, public sector or private, for profit or not for profit, needs to implement each of the 14 Infosec Basics. You do not need to take time out to do a formal risk assessment prior to implementing them. You've read Chapter 1 of this book, and you've recognized that there are a number of general threats to your business and its information, and you've recognized that you have a range of compliance obligations, and you've formed the view that your infrastructure is inadequate to meet those threats and obligations. You will already be doing some of the basics, but not necessarily all of them, and not necessarily any of them well enough. At this point, that's enough of a risk assessment.

So, if all the Infosec Basics are not in place, you should move quickly to implement as many of them as are missing and before you even think about how you are going to do the more formal risk assessment. The Infosec Basics for Business really are that basic. Here they are:

1. Have a policy.
2. Insist on accountability and responsibility.
3. Identify asset ownership and classification.
4. Address information security in contracts: all employment and third-party contracts must include information security.
5. Provide for the physical security of information systems.
6. Have up-to-date anti-malware software.
7. Implement and enforce user access controls.
8. Implement and enforce system access controls.
9. Manage vulnerabilities.
10. Have an incident response process.
11. Have basic business continuity and disaster recovery plans.
12. Monitor compliance.
13. Document essential policies, processes and procedures.
14. Ensure that users are trained and aware of their responsibilities.

Larger, more complex organizations will need to go substantially beyond the Infosec Basics, and Chapter 6 looks at some of the specific needs of larger organizations, including the deployment of BS 7799/ISO 17799. The needs of smaller organizations, which have specific issues around resource allocation and getting the blend between business security and customer responsiveness right, are addressed in Chapter 5.

The Infosec Basics provide guidance for an organizational response to information security threats. All employees have a specific role to play in that response, and guidelines for their response are in the Internet Highway Code. The Infosec Basics do not repeat any of that guidance and it is assumed that the organization will issue all its computer users with a copy of the Internet Highway Code or some similar guidance.

IMPLEMENTATION GUIDANCE

There are five areas on which the board's focus needs to be quite specific. The level of attention for each area will of course depend on the size of the company and the complexity of the threats and risks it faces:

1. The information security policy (of which more below) is the critical starting point. The board must ensure that one is drawn up, ensure that it is real, practical and reflects the business model and strategic business objectives, and must then visibly and unmistakably get behind implementing it. This, board commitment and leadership, is the *sine qua non* of an ISMS implementation: with them, the business will become secure; without them, it's almost not worth bothering. And by 'board commitment', what is meant is an informed, strategic, focused ownership of and ultimate accountability for the success of the information security strategy with a level of commitment that is no less than that given to, for instance, the sales strategy. By 'leadership', what is meant is giving a clear direction to the organization, setting the pace, and 'walking the talk', being an exemplar of the security practices that have been mandated.

2. The board must allocate resources and responsibilities – ensuring that adequately qualified individuals have adequate resources and clear objectives, which, together, will enable the security policy to be implemented. Objectives should be clearly and uncompromisingly communicated from the top down, and it should be clear that each individual will be held to account for delivery. Of course, identifying, agreeing and providing the necessary resources to do the job is at least as important. This includes making decisions about the extent to which external expertise is required – and, in general, it makes sense to bring in outside support that can quickly help raise the level of knowledge and expertise inside the organization while at the same time assisting in the design and implementation of an appropriate ISMS. Outside help is not, however, essential.

3. The board is responsible for project initiation and for ensuring that the project delivers its objectives – ensuring that the development and implementation of the Infosec Basics or a more sophisticated Information Security Management System proceeds in line with a clearly thought-through, pragmatic plan. Of course, this means there must be a plan in the first place: the project management approach and

methodology will depend on the scale and complexity of the organization.

There are two key criteria for deciding on the most effective approach to implementation: the Infosec Basics need to be rolled out quickly and methodically. There needs to be just enough time for everyone who needs to be involved in the decision-making process to make a contribution, but insufficient time for them to slow down or halt the project. If possible, one person should have the authority to push it through, subject to monitoring by the board and the executives (see Infosec Basic 2, below). The areas from which resistance may come include the IT department, who might not like losing control of something they enjoy and that gives them power over others. You should be prepared to replace those IT staff that cannot get behind the notion of a transparent, controlled, business-driven Information Security Management System. Of course, you should have a similar approach to line managers who think that securing the enterprise is somehow less important than anything else.

Of course, attention must also be paid to those basics of effective management: communication, managing change and budget control. Documentation (see Infosec Basic 13) will be essential and the organization can either create its own from scratch or buy a downloadable set of policy templates that can be easily adapted for deployment. The website, www.itgovernance.co.uk, has a set of templates designed to fit with the guidance in this book. If the organization already operates other management quality assurance systems (such as ISO 9000), consideration should be given to how the Infosec Basics will integrate into the existing processes.

Finally, there is the question of prioritization. It is possible that you will already have some of these controls in place, and you have only limited resources with which to tackle this project. The 'quick and dirty' approach to implementing the Infosec Basics is to ensure that the basic perimeter defences are in place before you do anything else. This can be done without much expense, and without needing to involve many people within the organization. The basic perimeter defences are Infosec Basic 6 (have up-to-date anti-malware software); Infosec Basic 9 (vulnerability management) and Infosec Basic 8 (have a firewall). Once those three controls are in place, the next to address are Infosec Basic 7 (have and enforce user access controls) and Infosec Basic 5 (provide for the physical security of information systems). Once you have these most basic of the basics in place, you can draw breath (only momentarily) before tackling the remaining Infosec Basics.

4. The board must approve, prior to implementation, each of the proposed controls, irrespective of whether they are technological or procedural. This is not difficult: all it requires is a process where those who

have been given the job of selecting and designing the controls have to demonstrate, to the board, how these controls will meet the various criteria that were set out in the information security policy at the outset of the project. The board satisfies itself that the criteria have really been met, that the criteria are still valid, and that no other previously unforeseen issues have been identified, and then gives the approval to go ahead. It is a good idea to keep a record of why the decision was made; that way, if you need to reconsider it later, you have all the original evidence still to hand.

5. As each control is successfully implemented, the board becomes re-sponsible for the ongoing, systematic monitoring of the performance of the Information Security Management System, ensuring that it remains up to date, effective and meets the policy objectives laid down for it. This is at least as important as the other four areas. Information security is a journey, not a destination. In fact, there is no destination. There needs to be a framework for monitoring and ensuring compli-ance and this starts with Infosec Basic 12.

Once the Infosec Basics are firmly in place, the board should – as described earlier – look at how it ensures that its future Information Security Manage-ment System will be proportionate to the risks it will face. This entails two further steps, both discussed in Chapter 2:

6. Risk assessment – identifying the strategic risks and risk categories that are likely to affect the business, and ensuring that, for each of the information assets (hardware, software, data, etc), there is a detailed risk assessment.
7. Risk treatment plan – setting the criteria by which risks are to be treated (accept, reject, transfer or accept but control) and, for those risks that are to be controlled, setting the criteria and standards that are to guide selection and implementation of the controls. These should, in simple terms, ensure that one doesn't spend more on con-trolling the risk than its likely impact.

Identify the scope of your project

Determining the scope of your information security project is harder for larger, complex organizations (see Chapter 6) than it is for smaller ones. It is, though, essential for any size of organization: you have to decide which information assets you're going to protect before you can decide on appropriate protection. This should be a quick decision for a small or medium-sized business: everything. That's because there will probably be hard-wired connections between all the information systems and day-to-day working relationships within the business that make it either extremely difficult or impractical to try to segregate one part of the business from another. The notion of segregation is at the heart of effective scoping: ultimately, you are going to try to create an impregnable barrier around that part of your business that is within the scope of your project and everything else. You have to be categorical about what is *inside* your information fortress and what is *outside*, and this means that you don't want *any* information systems, devices or business units that are *both* inside and outside – because *that* will be your weakest link.

In today's business environment, your defensive barrier has to operate at the individual device level and is highly dependent on user compliance with business procedures. In other words, your scoping decision needs to include all the information devices that people use in their jobs – such as cellphones, PDAs, wireless laptops, home offices, etc – as well as the more obvious central office systems – accounting, payment processing, production, sales and order management, e-mail, office automation, etc.

In larger, more complex businesses, you will also want to ensure that the entity that is within scope has a clearly defined legal and management structure and that there is alignment with the compliance requirements – part of the reason for your information security system is to ensure that you are compliant with the myriad of laws and regulations, so it makes sense for that entity that has those compliance obligations, to be fully within the scope of your information security project.

It helps (but is not essential) to make a simple network map that shows how your central systems link together and which identifies all of the points at which the outside world can interact with your network. This map will be very simple for a small organization and far more complex for a larger organization. There is a range of network mapping software that will automatically map your network for you, some of which have additional management features added in. The benefit of using such a tool is that it will quickly, completely and competently identify for you how your network is structured, what types of services are running and what access points and devices there actually are – and a status report of what is actually happening is much more useful than relying on a theoretical map.

Network maps are often drawn using software tools such as SmartDraw and Microsoft Visio, although one can start with a whiteboard and hand-draw a network diagram before attempting to model it with a software tool. Your network map wants to identify all the devices (for example, workstations 4, **servers** 2) that are connected to it, as well as their functions (for example, print and file server, domain controller, etc), their model and manufacturer details (for example, Toshiba Portege, Dell Poweredge), key specifications (RAM, processor speed, etc), their operating systems (for example, Windows XP), the applications they run (for example, Office

2003, Server 2003, Anti-virus 2005) and the nature of the physical connections between them (for example, Ethernet, Cat 5 cable, wireless, T1 line). Remember that your map should include all devices that are fixed to computers, such as hubs, routers, switches, backup units, RAID controllers, etc) and should, if possible, include the manufacturer's serial numbers of the devices. Figure 4.1 is an example of a simple network map, produced in SmartDraw, showing some of the information types identified above. It clearly identifies two points at which the firewall is bypassed (the wireless hub and the remote access **port**), as well as some of the mission critical devices (the 24-port hub, as well as the primary domain controller, for instance). Larger networks will have more complex maps, an example of which is included in Chapter 6.

The network map should integrate with the technology asset list and should be a live document, which is updated as and when the network is changed. It is also one of the most sensitive documents that any organization possesses, so it should be under **document control** and have a high security classification.

Once you have a clear diagram, or map, of your network(s), together with a list of all the assets that you want to be within the scope of your protective efforts, you can get on with the first Infosec Basic, the policy statement.

1. Have a policy

Every organization needs a basic statement from its board, which sets out the overall policy for securing the availability, confidentiality and integrity of the organization's information assets and which reflects senior management's commitment to it. Creating this policy may be an iterative process (particularly in complex organizations dealing with complex information security issues and/or multiple domains) and the final form of security policy that is adopted may only emerge after the final risk assessment has been carried out. What we need initially is a policy statement that creates the overall framework for action, or which pulls current information security activity and requirements into a coherent framework.

An information security policy answers the four key questions: who, where, what and why? Who is responsible for information security in the organization? To which parts of the organization does the policy apply? What are we required to do? And why are we required to do it?

An Infosec Basics policy statement should require no more than a single side of A4. It might say:

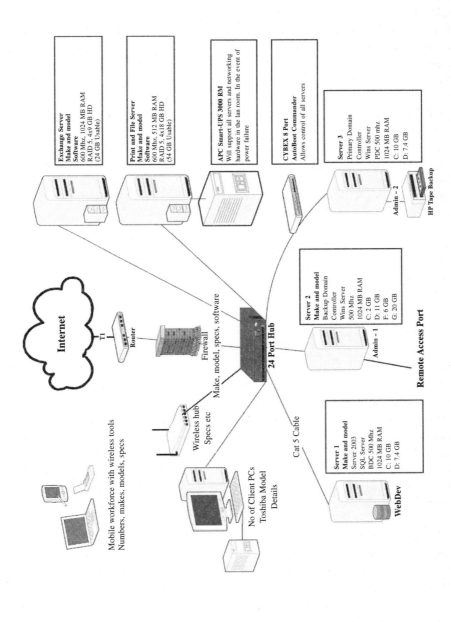

Figure 4.1 Simple network map produced in SmartDraw

The board and management of organization Y, which operates in sector Z (or is in the business of Z, etc), located in [ ], are committed to preserving the availability, confidentiality, and integrity of all the physical and electronic information assets in the organization in order to maintain its competitive edge, cash-flow, profitability, legal and contractual compliance and commercial image. Information and information security requirements will continue to be aligned with organizational goals. All employees of the organization are required to be accountable for the information assets for which they are responsible, to comply with this policy and with the procedures and guidelines that implement this policy, and will receive appropriate security training. Third parties who connect to our systems or deal with our information will also be required to comply with it. Once we are satisfied that we have achieved an adequate level of information security, we will implement a process of risk assessment and risk treatment that enables us to identify the further steps we need to take.

The policy statement should specifically reference the assets and entity that have been identified as being within the scope of the project.

In addition, the policy should state the organization has the following specific compliance requirements: information systems and assets must be kept physically secure; up-to-date anti-malware and firewall software is required; users are required to conform with company rules on access to information systems and assets; software must be approved by the company and all updates implemented; all staff must comply with the security incident reporting procedure; rules about backup, continuity planning and business continuity plans must be observed; and that the organization will take steps to ensure that its policy is observed. It would probably be sensible to attach a list of definitions for the key terms, such as those highlighted above. A template for this policy, and for other guidelines that will be required, are all accessible through www.itgovernance. co.uk.

This policy document should be drawn up, agreed by the board, signed and dated by the Chief Executive, issued to every member of staff and posted on notice boards – or, if you use an intranet, there. If you wanted to be precise, you would also make it a **controlled document**.

2.   Insist on accountability and responsibility

The board must do three things:

a)   Identify who, on the board and in the senior management team, is accountable for ensuring that the organization's information assets are secure.

b) Insist that everyone inside the organization accepts individual responsibility, which is related to their function and seniority, for their part in the information security activities. This includes ensuring that all directors, managers and supervisors clearly understand the importance to the organization of information security and that their full, informed and enthusiastic support is both required and expected.

c) Appoint someone to be the organization's information security expert (and the extent of the role depends on the complexity of the organization). For preference, these responsibilities should all be confirmed in writing to the individuals concerned.

The executive who has the accountability for information security is the person who will ensure, on behalf of the board, that the project is driven to conclusion, within the agreed time frame and budget, and that challenges and problems are overcome. A 'can do' attitude, some ruthlessness and the full support of the CEO are the essentials that will create someone who will be successful in this role. Two key processes that this person needs to set up and agree with the board are:

a) The process for approving controls prior to their implementation, to ensure that they are in line with the organization's requirements. This can be a very simple procedure during implementation of the Infosec Basics, restricted to providing clear evidence that the solution selected meets performance and cost requirements and that there was a proper selection process.

b) The process for approving changes to controls is more important. Once the basics are in place, you want to be sure that all changes (especially implementation of new controls) take the organization forward and address real organizational priorities.

Employment contracts will need to be amended to contain a clear statement that employees are expected to comply with the information security policy and any procedures issued under it and will specifically be expected to comply with the terms of any **access agreement** or acceptable use policy (both of which are addressed in Infosec Basic 7) that the employer expects them to sign.

The organization's information security expert could be an insider or an outsider. There are arguments for both. What is important is the existence of someone who understands the information security issues and processes, who can communicate clearly with people at all levels of the business, and who can ensure that individual information security incidents are properly dealt with. This is a middle (or, in larger organizations, a senior) management position, not a purely technical one. Technical expertise would be helpful in this role, but attributes such as communication skills, **forensic** skills and a methodological approach are at least as import-ant. This person needs to have access to regular information about security issues and should be receiving regular alerts (such as the one available from IT Governance or those from other information services) on urgent information security issues that are relevant to your business. Sooner or later, you will want the person in this role to obtain an appropriate qualifi-cation. You will also need to ensure, in the longer term, that you have appropriate succession plans in place to cover this person's departure.

3.   Identify asset ownership and classification

Ownership

This requirement is simple to describe, but quite time-consuming to imple-ment. 'Assets', for the purposes of this section, is a key area. You need to create a full inventory of the organization's information assets, looking at each of the categories identified in the definition. The network map and physical asset list that you produced in the initial scoping exercise is the starting point for this exercise. Hopefully, you agreed the network map-derived asset list to the finance department's fixed asset register, to ensure that there were no missing assets on either register. Now you need to extend the list to cover all the categories of information asset. This is an exercise in which it is 'better to be approximately correct than absolutely wrong'; in other words, if you've identified approximately 80 per cent of the assets, including all the most important ones, you've made a good enough start on securing your business.

Each of your information assets should have an identified owner and this person's name should be recorded on the asset list (which must therefore be kept up to date to reflect changes in staffing, job roles, etc). Clearly, the 'owner' is the person, or function, that has responsibility for the asset – the 'owner' has no property rights to the asset. The owner is responsible for ensuring that the Infosec Basics that are relevant to their asset(s) are applied. This responsibility should be clearly communicated to every owner, and written into their access agreements and the accept-able use policy. In terms of desktop computers, laptops, cellphones, etc, the owner will be the person to whom they are assigned and who generally uses them.

Usually, whoever is responsible for the facilities management in the organization will be the nominated owner of the relevant services and a number of the physical assets. The IT Manager will usually be responsible for the other physical assets and the majority of the software, although individual users should be responsible for the software on the laptop or cellphone or any other, similar, item that they have been assigned.

It is much more difficult to determine the owners of the intangible information assets. In terms of new information (whether digital or analogue), the organization could simply adopt the policy that the originator will be defined as its owner. This is meaningful in terms of information assets that will have, generally, a specific and limited use, and which is driven by the originator. This would cover, for instance, business plans, forecasts, client letters and project plans, etc.

The use of other information assets can, however, be widespread through the organization and which will have been acquired as the result of a strategic or group decision. Examples might include Customer Relationship Management (CRM) systems and their client data, workflow systems and the information they contain, accounting systems and financial information. The only practical approach to these assets is for the organization to nominate as its owner the person who (or whose department) uses it the most, or has most control over it: for instance, the financial controller might be the nominated owner of the accounting system and the sales administrator might be the nominated owner of the CRM system.

One issue that often arises at this point is the fact that a number of illicit software packages are found to be running on corporate computers. For instance, the organization has licences for 120 copies of Windows XP and it proves (with laptops and so on) to be running 174 of them – that's 54 illegal copies of software. Many workstations will also prove to be running software that may, or may not, be shareware or freeware (which you may or may not want). Every software copy for which you cannot prove proper ownership is potentially an illegal copy. A number of organizations exist specifically to target illegal copying; they encourage whistle-blowing and they have a programme of targeting potential perpetrators. Fines and reputation damage can follow.

Many instances of illegal copying arise accidentally; the organization has grown quickly, or systems have been upgraded, and the growth in the number of instances of each software package has been uncontrolled. It's simple to put right and cheaper to do so at once. You reduce the number of installed instances of each item of software to the necessary level, and you buy additional licences for whatever the excess number over your existing licence base is. Thereafter, you keep a software register, which you update for new computer deployments, and you buy the additional licences you need as and when you need them. You include, in the user agreements, a ban on the installation on corporate computers of unlicensed software, and you have your internal audit team to do regular audits of this.

Classification

This is a subject that can be complex, and in complex organizations, it probably needs to be. *IT Governance: A Manager's Guide to Data Security and BS 7799/ISO 17799* contains an extensive review of information (or document) classification systems. What we need, though, is something basic and straightforward that can be applied to all the organization's information assets, both digital and analogue, so that everyone knows what the appropriate treatment for each item might be. Document classifications should be included in the document header, and should be set to appear on all pages of the document. The classification system should be described on a single sheet of paper and issued to all staff. It will also have relevance, in due course, for ensuring that information security levels are appropriate for the value of the asset at risk, particularly in terms of access controls, which are covered in Infosec Basic 7.

The simplest approach is usually one that has only three levels of classification. The first level identifies information that is so confidential that it has to be restricted to the board and specific professional advisers. Information that falls into this category is marked 'Highly Confidential', with the names of the people to whom it is restricted identified on the document. Examples of highly confidential information might include information about potential acquisitions or corporate strategy, or about key organizational personnel, such as the chief executive. The amount of information that falls into this category should be carefully limited; the cost and operational inconvenience of protecting it properly is such that it needs only to be information whose release can significantly damage the organization.

A second level of classification should cover documents that are to be available only to senior or other specified levels of management within the organization. These might be marked 'Confidential – Restricted'. Examples might include draft statutory accounts, which might be available to everyone in senior management, or implementation plans for corporate restructuring, which senior managers need to work through prior to their being rolled out.

The final level of classification is: 'Confidential' and this should cover everything that has value, which should not be allowed to fall into the hands of third parties, but does not fit within either of the other two categories. Every employee should be entitled to access information with this classification.

4. Address information security in contracts

All contracts – employment contracts, outsourcing contracts, third-party contracts, and customer contracts, need to deal with information security issues. This will take a considerable time – and the input from your corporate lawyers – to prepare and roll out. The two most important areas are employment and outsourcing – approximately half of all information security incidents are caused by INSIDERS, employees or contractors – and so these must be tackled as a priority. Obviously, existing contracts will need to be updated, but it may not be possible to do this immediately. New starters and new outsourcing contracts must be drafted so that they set out clearly the individual or the supplier's information security responsibilities. Once steps have been taken to deal with new contracts, a robust approach must be taken to dealing with the existing ones. Suppliers and employees will need different strategies.

Outsource suppliers

Any organization that takes over and supplies key services is likely to be an outsourcing company. Insofar as the outsourcing company has responsibility for organizational data (a call centre, for instance, or a payroll bureau, both of which may be collecting personal data and both of which may be interacting with organizational information systems), the consequent risks need to be addressed in the outsourcing contract. In a nutshell, you should want your outsourcing company to maintain information security controls that will at least match those you require of yourself. Appropriate clauses should be drafted by your corporate lawyers and, if they haven't had experience of information security in outsourcing arrangements, find a specialist firm. Your definition of 'outsourcing company' should be expanded to include contractors (for instance, IT contractors), interim managers, consultants, facilities and security staff, and cleaners – anyone who is dealing with your information assets, your information systems, or who might have access to them, but who isn't an employee, should be captured by your definition.

Employees

You need to address information security at three stages of employment: recruitment, during employment and at termination. You will need to take the specific advice of your employment lawyers to ensure that your procedures comply with local law, but you want to be sure that you can screen employees for sensitive positions prior to appointing them; that you can require specific compliance behaviour from them during employment (and these are set out in Infosec Basic 7, below), and that upon termination you can enforce confidentiality clauses and get all information and other assets returned. Your disciplinary policy will also need to be upgraded so that it specifically deals with breaches of information security policy and guidelines.

Other third parties

There are many other third parties that might from time to time need to see – or access – confidential information. You should have a standard **non-disclosure agreement** (**NDA**) drafted by your lawyers, which is available for use at any time. Its information security clauses should, to the greatest extent possible, be consistent with those in your employment and outsourcing contracts. You should not reveal confidential information without first having had a copy of the NDA signed and returned to you. If you are a private sector firm contracting with the public sector, you need to think through how you want to handle the possible implications of the Freedom of Information Act.

5. Provide for the physical security of information systems

There are two aspects to this: desktop systems and central systems. The latter is more important for organizational security than the former, and the former can be dealt with through a combination of ensuring that all users are familiar with the guidance of principle 1 of the Internet Highway Code and ensuring that desktop computers in the workplace have been safely set up: on a stable base, with cables controlled with cable tidies so that they can't trip people or get pulled out accidentally (sometimes they pull the computer over as well!). Dealing with physical security includes ensuring making life difficult for thieves: laptops should be cable-tied during the day and locked in a laptop safe at night – or taken home, as discussed in Chapter 7. Don't pile up empty computer boxes outside the front door after unpacking a load of new computers: it only attracts thieves. Above all, have your insurance company and the local police service assess any risks to your premises and provide advice on how best to secure against them. Of course, you should make sure that all your information systems are properly covered by insurance and that you are aware of any exclusions in the terms of that cover.

Central systems are the heart of the organization's information operation. Traditionally, all the corporate servers on which the organization's applications all run are set up in a central server room. The server room is usually the responsibility of the Head of IT. Basic security measures for this central server room are:

a) It should not be possible for anyone outside the room to see what is inside it.

b) The entrance to the room should be in a highly visible, well-lit area that is regularly monitored, so that any unauthorized ingress attempt is immediately obvious.

c) The room should be physically secure: strong walls, floor and roof, with a solid door, substantial locks and an automatic door closer. Power cable supplies should, if possible, be secure – so that someone can't access them to cut them or to gain ingress to the servers. The room should have a password-protected entry system; the password should be changed regularly and should only be known to those who have to be in the room. Visitors should not be given the password, but be accompanied at all times by someone who is authorized to enter.

d) All the equipment should be racked, with safe cabling, so that it is easy to get to each device.

e) The room should be tidy, free from clutter, junk, manuals, food, drink, etc.

f) The room will certainly need to be air conditioned (fans aren't that good at removing the heat generated by a bunch of servers) and may need an emergency lighting service, and fire suppression equipment – although that will depend on the level of risk related to the information on the systems.

g) UPS equipment will be necessary for all the equipment in the server room. This should be appropriately rated for the devices plugged into them and should provide surge protection as well as enough battery-operated power for the servers to shut down properly in the event of a power failure. The UPS equipment should be tested IN ACTION regularly.

6. Have up-to-date anti-malware software

Viruses

Anti-virus software is no longer enough. Blended threats are increasingly an issue, as is spyware. Viruses and worms continue to evolve. Spam continues to proliferate. Organizations, therefore, need to deploy industrial strength ('enterprise editions') versions of anti-malware software that has at least the following characteristics:

a) It should work across the whole organization, and on all software and hardware platforms, and on all workstations and servers.

b) It should be scalable, to handle future growth.

c) It should supply centralized administration: configuration, deployment, management, updating, reporting.
d) It should have automatic updates, preferably daily – it's no good having a week-long wait for protection for a newly released virus.
e) It should ensure that remote (teleworker or mobile) devices connecting to the network are compliant – that is, have up-to-date anti-virus software.
f) It should have **heuristic** capability as well as a database of virus signatures
g) It should be integrated with the anti-spam tool and possibly the firewall.

All of this means that the number of potential providers will be small; you want to be sure that the provider you choose has an established reputation for upgrading its software quickly enough to stay in touch with the rapidly evolving range of threats.

You should remember that anti-virus software also needs to be deployed to all teleworkers, mobile workers, wireless laptops, handheld computers, PDAs and cellphones. All are possible virus attack vectors, and your corporate security is only as strong as your weakest link.

You should subscribe to an alert service, preferably one that will aggregate information from a number of sources and will alert you to emerging threats and newly identified vulnerabilities across a range of operating systems and devices (that is, cellphones, PDAs, computer systems, spyware, viruses, worms, vulnerabilities, etc). These services may have to be paid for.

User training is an essential part of an effective anti-malware posture: users must know how to respond to virus hoaxes, about not opening e-mails from unknown/unexpected sources, etc. The Internet Highway Code provides essential user guidance on this and should be in the hands of all employees. Your policy requirements around anti-virus software (that it must be updated, that it may never be switched off) should also be written into the user agreement.

Spam

Spam is a curse; it is also sometimes positive, useful advertising. Organizations need ways of rejecting the former but allowing in the latter. This depends on a combination of enterprise-level software and individual-level training. The enterprise-level software (which should, for ease of administration be integrated with the anti-virus software), should have the ability to filter out all known spammers and all e-mails that have the characteristics of spam. It should also be possible for users to add to the corporate whitelist those sites and senders from whom they want to receive e-mails, or many legitimate and desired e-mails sent by automated webmailing systems (such as alert letters from anti-virus companies) will be treated as spam and blocked at the gateway.

User training is an essential part of the war against spam; user dos and don'ts are covered in the Internet Highway Code principle 6.

Spyware

Spyware is more complex. At the time of writing this book, no anti-virus vendor had a complete anti-spyware package that integrated with its anti-virus software. Spyware's attack vector is different from that of viruses: it is usually downloaded (intentionally or unintentionally) from a website. Updates on developments in this area may be found at www.itgovernance. co.uk, but you should assume that you should deploy an anti-spyware package to every computer and have it set to automatic detection and update. Microsoft's anti-spyware is one such tool, and can be downloaded from the Microsoft website. User training is an essential component of dealing with spyware, and this is covered in Internet Highway Code principle 7.

7.   Implement and enforce user access controls

User names, rights and privileges

While it is unlikely that any business computer system does not allocate individual user names to employees and others, not all organizations have a clear security policy for how this should be done. At the basic level, user names should be unique, allocated to individuals and subject to a signed user agreement; it should be a disciplinary offence for anyone to use someone else's user name. Using someone else's user name is identity theft and any multi-user systems set up to require only one user name are exposing themselves to untraceable abuse. People who do not need access to specific systems should not be given access to them and deployment of **single sign-on** systems provide an opportunity to configure user access rights appropriately. The asset list created at the implementation stage of the project can help make decisions about the role and level of employees who should have access to each system. Group IDs and the '**guest**' user name should not be available for use: administrators should be issued with standard user names for their everyday work and only use their own administrator name when they have a specific system administrative task to perform. AS SOON AS (not three months later) someone leaves the organization or their role changes, their user name must be withdrawn or their user rights amended to reflect the new circumstances.

Privileges should only be allocated to specific users when they are needed, and withdrawn as soon as they are no longer needed. No amount of brow-beating by IT staff should lead a business manager to any other action; if someone does not actually need a specific power or right, then don't give it to them: what someone doesn't have can't be exploited.

Passwords

Organizations should deploy central system management software that enforces password changes and which requires them to be good quality: seven or more characters long, alpha-numeric, enforced change every 30 days, no reuse of passwords and no use of sequential passwords (for example, rogerson1, rogerson2, etc). User guidance on password selection is in Internet Highway Code principle 2.

The user agreement should state the rules on password selection, and set out the requirement for confidentiality, for temporary passwords to be changed at first logon, and that individuals may not share their passwords – or divulge them to anyone, however strong the argument is that they do so (see social engineering).

Users should be required to have a password-protected screensaver (see Internet Highway Code principle 2).

There are organizations for whom strong, **two-factor authentication** will be a must, but that is a need more advanced than an Infosec Basic.

User agreements and acceptable use policies

User agreements and acceptable use policies have two fundamental purposes: to explain clearly to users what rights and responsibilities they have in relation to the organizational systems, and to create the legal basis for taking action against those employees (or third party contractors) who abuse these rights or fail in these responsibilities.

The user agreement should contain the employee's allocated user name and:

a) details of user access rights;
b) details of any privileges granted;
c) requirements for password structures;
d) requirements for password-protected screensavers, and for powering off when not using the computer;
e) requirement not to download or install any unauthorized software;
f) requirement for authorization from the organization's **Data Controller** for storage of any **personal data**;
g) requirements in terms of firewalls (Infosec Basic 8), incident response (Infosec Basic 10), vulnerabilities (Infosec Basic 9) and backing up information (Infosec Basic 11);

h) requirement to abide by the acceptable use policy; and

i) should set out clearly how the organization's disciplinary policy (set up with the assistance of your employment lawyers) will be deployed to deal with users who breach the terms of their user agreement.

The acceptable use policy is an organization-wide policy that defines what will be considered acceptable use of the organization's computer systems, particularly e-mail and internet access. Apart from the cost of corporate **bandwidth** and the use of employee time, the risks – and repercussions for the organization – of inappropriate use of e-mail or of internet surfing are severe and should be controlled. The development of an acceptable use policy is, in the United Kingdom, subject to law and is relatively complex. Development and deployment of an acceptable use policy is beyond the scope of this book; there is a substantial chapter on it in *IT Governance: A Manager's Guide to Data Security and BS 7799/ISO 17799*, and a downloadable toolkit for acceptable use policies is available from www. itgovernance.co.uk. Employees should also be expected to follow the guidance in Internet Highway Code principle 8.

8. Implement and enforce system access controls

Firewalls

The first and most important system access control is the one that controls access to the corporate network: the firewall. Firewalls (combination standalone server with up-to-date firewall software, configured in line with corporate policy about what internet access should be allowed, with the administrator user name and password changed so that they are in line with the corporate password policy) have now become standard technology and are essential between the corporate network and the internet. The key issue around network access control is to identify all the routes into the network that will bypass the firewall and to deal with those. Two of the most usual ways of bypassing the firewall are through wireless networking and through remote access ports. The firewall also needs to be regularly tested by a third party penetration testing company, whose recommendations should (unless they conflict with business object-ives) be implemented.

Workstations within the network will not need their own machine-level firewalls; mobile workers, teleworkers and all laptops should have machine-level firewalls that will not compete with the corporate one.

Firewalls are also used to separate internal systems, to create secure extranets, or to create **DMZs** (demilitarized zones) outside the secure corporate network. These more complex **architectures** are important for larger organizations and are beyond the scope of this chapter.

System logon

Login to individual systems should be controlled through the organization's single sign-on software, which should be configured in line with user access rights. The system logon screen should also be configured to limit opportunities for unauthorized users to fraudulently authenticate themselves. System administrators should configure all logon screens so that they:

a) display no system identifiers until the logon process has been completed successfully;
b) display no help messages during the process – authorized users are supposed to know how to logon;
c) only validate the data on completion of the logon and, if it is incorrect, reject it without explanation and require complete re-input;
d) limit the number of unsuccessful logon attempts to three, after which they are locked out and have to contact the administrator;
e) limit the maximum time for successful logon to five minutes.

9. *Manage vulnerabilities*

Vulnerabilities are exploited by threats. All software has vulnerabilities and, as soon as a new one is identified and announced, there is a race between the criminal community and the software company to deal with it. The software company needs to patch the vulnerability before the criminals can exploit it. **Bugtraq** and **CVE** (Common Vulnerabilities and Exposures website) are the best places for the criminals to get updates about vulnerabilities. Vulnerabilities are how criminals (hackers, virus writers, scumware writers, spammers, spies and criminals) can get into your systems, steal your data and disrupt your operation. PATCHING VULNERABILITIES IS PROBABLY THE MOST IMPORTANT AND BASIC INFORMATION SECURITY STEP THAT ANY ORGANIZATION CAN TAKE. Without vulnerabilities, there wouldn't be hackers and viruses.

Smaller organizations can deal with this simply by subscribing to the automatic update services of their software providers and ensuring that the updates actually run. (User agreements should expressly require users never to turn off or interfere with the automatic update facility.) Medium-sized and large organizations that are deploying a number of applications on (perhaps) more than one operating system need to ensure that all vulnerabilities are identified and patched. This is something that needs to be done on a regular basis. The best way to deal with this is to acquire and deploy **vulnerability scanning** software, that has regular updates from Bugtraq and CVE, and which can be set to run on a regular basis. It is essential that, when vulnerabilities are detected, the recommended patches are installed as quickly as possible. If there is any question about the order in which vulnerabilities should be addressed, the **SANS top 20** can answer it.

Larger organizations with more complex systems, particularly those with bespoke software, may need to test patches (to ensure they don't affect any other systems) before deploying them. This needs to be done in a proper test environment, which is running a duplicate of the systems for which the patch is being tested. Unless there is a similarly good reason for testing prior to release, patches should be installed as soon as they become available.

10. Have an incident response process

Information security defences evolve to meet information security threats. That means that the threats are in the driving seat, and your defences are only responses to them. Therefore, however good your information security defences are, sooner or later something will get through. The likelihood of this is greater if you only have a basic ISMS than if you have a sophisticated, well-established one.

You need, therefore, an organizational process for responding to information security incidents in order to limit business disruption. In essence, the process you need to roll out has two elements: what users should do when something unexpected happens, and how these events should be dealt with.

Users throughout the organization should be taught that, if something unusual happens to their computer, it might actually be a problem and that they shouldn't try to resolve it themselves – even if they think they caused it. Instead, they should step back from their computer, call whoever is designated as the information security incident response person, and then watch and note what is happening on the screen until help arrives.

The organization's information security specialist is probably best suited to this role. As soon as s/he is on the scene, the incident can be dealt with. It may be necessary to disconnect the computer from the network until the matter is dealt with and the user's observations will help make this decision. The technical staff deal with the computer, ensure that it is running according to specification, and then re-attach it to the network.

Of course, in recruiting an information security expert, it makes sense to get someone who knows how to distinguish between viruses, worms, Trojans and hacker intrusions, who knows how to clean up a PC and also knows how to restore it and the system. The event could also be a technical fault and, therefore, the information security adviser must be able to

differentiate attacks from faults and have an established method for dealing with the latter. If the incident points to ways in which information
security can be improved, appropriate and immediate action should be
taken to implement these improvements.

This simple incident response process should be written into staff user
agreements. Larger organizations need a more sophisticated process, but
its elements are exactly the same.

11. Have basic business continuity and disaster recovery plans

The difference between these two is this: a business continuity plan is
essential on a day-to-day basis, a disaster recovery plan is essential for
recovering from 'acts of nature'. The two should go hand in hand; in a
very real sense, business continuity depends on being able to recover from
disasters in a way that is relatively seamless. The basic business continuity
and disaster recovery requirements for any organization are these:

a) Backup – the central servers must be backed up at least every night.
   (Some very important information might need backing up more regularly, but that is a risk assessment decision for each organization.)
   The backup is probably to Digital Audio Tape (DAT); a proper **backup
   cycle** should be applied and the tapes should be stored offsite. Backup
   tapes should have the same level of protection as the original data –
   they are just as valuable.

b) Information stored on workstation C: drives must also be backed up.
   Central backup technology, which is backing up the server, can't also
   back up the workstations. Users must therefore be taught to save all-
   important documents to their personal folders in the corporate shared
   drives; this should also be covered in user agreements.

c) Information stored on laptops, PDAs and cellphones must also be
   backed up. PDAs and cellphones should be backed up to their host
   workstations or laptops. Laptops should be backed up by the users,
   either whenever they logon to the system (following the same requirements as users of fixed workstations) or there should be an appropriate online (web-based) backup service available.

d) Recovery and restoration from backup should be tested so that, should
   the need arise, users and network administrators know how to do it
   and any additional devices that might turn out to be required for the
   process can be acquired in advance of their being needed.

e) Power is the other key continuity issue. All essential business services
   (which are likely to include telephones, servers, network computers,

and so on – although each business needs to make a conscious choice about what is, and what isn't, essential) must have a UPS. The UPS must be tested on a regular basis, and you will want to be sure that it will in fact provide sufficient power to allow an orderly shutdown of the services it supports.

f)   Have a basic plan for what you would do if an 'act of nature' did happen to your business. Decide how you will run your business, from where and with what. If, after a few minutes of thinking about this, you realize how terminal an act of nature could be, you might start looking at developing a real disaster recovery plan.

12.   Monitor compliance

Information security threats are continually evolving and the risk environment is different month to month and year to year. Legal requirements (for example, data protection, privacy, computer misuse, all as discussed in Chapter 9) don't decrease. Your staff is also always changing, and the average company will experience 25 per cent staff turnover every year. Technology keeps advancing, competitors come and go, and customer demands never reduce. Taken together, these factors mean that:

a)   Your defences have to continually evolve to meet the most recent threats or cover the latest vulnerabilities.

b)   You need an ongoing monitoring programme to ensure that the controls you implemented are still in place, that technology is performing in line with requirements (that is, are anti-virus updates being downloaded, are software patches being installed?) and that staff are still performing in line with expectations (that is, does the new IT Manager follow the correct backup procedure, does the new sales team understand how to secure their wireless communications, did the outgoing accounts clerk sabotage the accounts system?).

c)   You must be sure that, across your business, everyone is complying with the requirements of the laws and regulations that affect your business; any failure by a single member of staff in this regard can create substantial expense for, and affect the reputation of, any organization and, increasingly, there are penalties for individual directors as well.

At a basic level, you need to expand the role of your internal audit team to cover the basic aspects of information security compliance. You will (following Infosec Basic 13, below) have documented the key policies and procedures, and your audit team should focus on checking for user compliance with their user agreements and the acceptable use policy, and that the system administrators are applying the requirements specifically identified for them in Infosec Basics 5, 6, 7, 8, 9 and 11. Your internal audit team is likely to need some training in order to carry out this responsibility.

The essential benefits of monitoring are threefold: you identify and can fix vulnerabilities before they are exploited; you send a warning to potential miscreants that they are likely to be caught; and you identify areas in which you can improve your security. While this is not a comprehensive audit and monitoring framework, it is a framework that will be initially adequate. In a more sophisticated or complex environment, you will want to substantially expand the range of audit activity.

13. Document essential policies and procedures

Documentation does not have to be extensive, but it does have to exist. Documentation serves three purposes: it enables you to apply a standard, thought-through methodology to dealing with specific information security events and situations (which provides continuity when you have staff changes); it gives you a baseline against which to plan detailed improvements; and it provides evidence, in industrial tribunal, criminal or civil courts, that you did have a standard procedure and that it was (or wasn't) complied with. The essential areas for documentation have been identified throughout this chapter and elsewhere in the book. You can develop your own set of documents in line with this guidance. You can also purchase a set of documents that reflect the Infosec Basics and which are compatible with ISO 17799 from www.itgovernance.co.uk.

14. Ensure that users are trained and aware of their responsibilities

Effective information security depends on a combination of procedural and technological controls as well as on individual user behaviour. It's rather like driving a car: however much we remove risk from the environment, an individual human being is going to be driving the computer into cyberspace. Adequate user training is, therefore, essential. It is also the area that most organizations do least well .

Information security training needs to have three components: users need to be competent to use their computers and to understand the requirements of their user agreements and the acceptable use policy; they need to recognize and know how to deal with information security threats; and they need to be kept aware of changes in the risk environment, so that they can take adequate evading action.

The Internet Highway Code is designed to meet the second need, and copies of it should be issued to all members of staff. User agreements could identify it and require staff to follow its guidelines. User agreements should be signed before users are issued with their user names; it should be crystal clear (that is, if evidence of acceptance of responsibility has to be produced in a tribunal or court of law, the user agreement is it) that users are aware of their responsibilities in relation to the corporate information systems. Computer training can be delivered through e-learning. User awareness can be delivered through an alert service, whether internally originated or externally sourced.

5

Essentials for smaller organizations

Chapter 4 looked at the state of information security management in many businesses today. Its guidance is appropriate for organizations that employ between about 150 people and several thousand. While smaller businesses (employing between 10 and 150 people) usually have fewer resources to target on information security than larger ones, they face many of the same threats. In fact, as was said in Chapter 4, 'the one area today in which businesses of all sizes enjoy a level playing field is in information security: ALL businesses are subject to world-class threats, all of them are potentially betrayed by world-class software vulnerabilities and all of them are subject to an increasingly complex set of (sometimes contradictory) computer- and privacy-related regulation'.

Information security is just as essential for the smaller business as it is for the large, complex ones. The reality is that, while smaller businesses are no less vulnerable than larger ones, they are less likely to have taken adequate steps to deal with those vulnerabilities. Information security breaches are also likely to disproportionately impact smaller businesses, which tend to be reliant on a small number of customers and dependent on a limited number of systems and processes.

The SOHO Internet Highway Code provides appropriate, initial guidance for individual business people and small office/home office networks. In real terms, there is an outside practical limit of 10 computers to the size of network for which that level of security guidance is adequate. Even at this level, the amount of work required for one individual to be responsible, whether for ensuring that all users are following the SOHO Internet Highway Code, or for applying to each computer the necessary controls, is too great to be practicable.

In any case, by the time an organization has 10 or so networked computers, it is already likely to have moved toward some form of centralized services (mail, file and print, accounting, customer management, etc) and it is for these organizations, who are most at risk from information security threats, and which probably have fewer than 150 employees, that this chapter is intended.

CHARACTERISTICS

This chapter sets out how an organization that has some or all of the characteristics listed below should approach deployment of the Infosec Basics for Business.

First of all, the business is likely to be 'owner managed'; in other words, its board and directors are likely also to be the majority shareholders in the business, and a substantial proportion of their personal wealth, as well as their income, is tied up in and dependent on, the business. It is likely to be very customer-focused business, and to pride itself on being nimble, responsive and unbureaucratic. It is likely to be very cost-conscious at quite a detailed level and is unlikely to carry much in the way of administrative overhead. It will, quite rightly, see computing as a business technology that should enhance and enable competitiveness and it is unlikely to be much interested in the detail of information security – even if, for a number of its client contracts, it has to demonstrate a certain level of compliance.

While the business may operate from more than one site, it is likely to have a single main office, which is where all its central services (as well as the directors) are based. It may have a number of employees who are either teleworkers or mobile workers. Depending on its business (and its size), it's likely to have a number of servers, in a central server room, and it's likely to be operating an increasingly wireless network, as well as running office automation software (Microsoft Office) and one or more applications (certainly including an accounting package, such as Sage or an equivalent, and perhaps sales automation software, and other specialist commercial off-the-shelf software). One or more of these packages may be on an **ASP (Application Service Provider)** basis, although that is unlikely. It is likely to be running a Windows environment (operating system), although some businesses may also have one or more Macs installed.

It is likely to have a website, although the hosting of this is likely to be outsourced. Increasingly, it's likely to be enjoying the cost benefit and flexibility of looking after its own website content maintenance. If it's operating an e-commerce business, the website will almost certainly be integrated with one of the third-party online payment services. It will almost certainly have a webmail service alongside the e-mail feed from its ISP to the Exchange **mail server**.

It is likely to buy its computers and related equipment from a (relatively) local computer supplier, who is likely to be an integrator (that is, integrates hardware and software from a number of different suppliers) and is likely to be responsible for cabling and second-line help-desk support.

Computer value-added resellers (**VAR**s) are not always information security experts. While they are likely to have a rudimentary knowledge of the subject, and a reasonable grasp of a number of the basics, they will certainly not have a sufficiently adequate understanding of each of their clients' businesses to be able to turn this basic grasp into a working ISMS.

Critically, a smaller business (unless its core business is e-commerce, or computer services or similar) is likely to have between one and four IT staff, one of whom is also the webmaster, responsible for managing the website and any e-commerce functionality. The IT team often reports to the Finance Director, because this is usually the person who is responsible for IT. Even though the management (including the Finance Director) and the rest of the staff are unlikely to have any personal knowledge or understanding of either computers or information security issues, these smaller businesses are sometimes on the cutting edge, introducing technologies that work in a domestic environment to their businesses because they are both simple and inexpensive to use. Invariably, information security requirements are not considered and, in general, information security is likely to be left to the IT team and to the computer supplier.

Unless the IT Manager has specific information security qualifications, this is an extremely dangerous situation for any business. If the IT Manager does have information security qualifications, the danger is lessened, but not enough for comfort. The reasons for the danger are clear:

1. The board and directors, who are legally accountable for compliance with local legislation and regulation, are unable to ensure that they are meeting their compliance requirements.

2. The board and directors, whose personal wealth and future earnings are often completely dependent on the business, are unable to ensure that the business will survive any one of the information security threats (see Chapters 1 and 4) out there.

3. In the vast majority of businesses of this size, neither the IT Manager nor the VAR is able to be properly aware of the business objectives or the business model, and it is therefore impossible for them to build an information security management system that will meet the organization's business needs.

4. The IT Manager is likely to be hard pushed to effectively manage the day-to-day central administration needs of the network, and this challenge becomes particularly acute whenever there are staff absences of any sort; this doesn't leave much time for considering, selecting, planning and implementing appropriate information security controls.

5. Whether or not he or she has information security qualifications, the IT Manager will recognize that he or she is far more experienced and knowledgeable than anyone else around computers, and will therefore tend to take the stance that he or she knows what does – and does not – need to be done. Experience teaches that, in these circumstances, whatever the IT Manager thinks needs to be done is not always that appropriate for the business.

6. In any case, it's just bad business practice to have only one person who can make the accounting, sales and other systems work, who is in a position to destroy or defraud the company, and over whom no controls, checks or balance are exercised.

IMPLEMENTATION ISSUES

Boards and managers have to make a conscious effort to tackle information security. The board needs to assess the threats and the organization's vulnerabilities. It needs to recognize that securing itself, at a basic level, against those threats will be neither disproportionately expensive nor time-consuming, but that it is essential.

The first step, therefore, is for one of the Executive Directors to accept personal responsibility – and accountability – for implementing the Infosec Basics for Business. We're not talking about BS 7799, or anything that might require substantial diversion of effort; we're talking about implementing the basics and doing them well. It's not unusual for the Finance Director or CFO to take on this responsibility; it is important that this person recognizes the time commitment, and that the board recognizes the need for this to come across to all employees as a business-driven project, not just a Finance and IT one.

The second step is to get the IT Manager and the other senior managers in the business on side. This book should help. The IT Manager needs to fully support the project, or you will need someone else in the role – after all, an IT Manager who is against an open, transparent, business-driven approach to information security is likely to have an agenda rather (and possibly maliciously) different from that of the owners and managers of the business.

Step three is to identify the gap between what you already have in place (and you will almost certainly have a number of the basics already in place) and what the Infosec Basics for Business recommend. The simplest way of tackling this is usually to map out each of the things that need to be done, tick off what has already been dealt with, assess whether or not it can be brought into line with what you are going to do and, if the answer is Yes, then get on with it.

If what has already been done can't be brought into line with what you need to do, the simplest approach is almost always to replace what you've got with what you need. The essential thing is to move with speed and determination to implement the Infosec Basics for Business as fast as possible.

Step four, therefore, is all about implementation. Your overall project plan should reflect the prioritization suggested in the implementation guidance section of Chapter 4. You should have user agreements drafted and ready to go at the outset of the project; remember to include a clause that clarifies that not all of the requirements will become operational simultaneously, but that employees will be expected to comply with them as soon as they are up and running. The IT team, on whom the initial workload will primarily fall, need clear instructions on what is required. You should map out with them the individual steps to get there, asking them for input on issues that may need to be resolved in the process. Agree a timetable for each of the actions, and monitor progress. Ensure that, for each of the Infosec Basics that has a procedural and a user element, you are in a position to roll out the related procedure and the user training when you make the technological changes – otherwise your business may come to a stop! Use third-party documentation – it's faster, less expensive and more comprehensive than trying to do it yourself. Buy in external expertise, to ensure that you're alerted to upcoming threats – it's cheaper and more reliable than trying to gather all the basic information yourself.

Step 4 is to recruit an information security expert. You could do this concurrently with one of the earlier steps. You should avoid recruiting an IT Manager who will also be your information security expert, not least because you do need a proper segregation of duties. You are unlikely, however, to need or afford such a person on a full-time basis. The logical way for you to deal with this need, therefore, will be to contract with an organization that can supply an information security partnering and mentoring service, which will give you the expertise when you need it.

SMALLER NOT-FOR-PROFIT ORGANIZATIONS

Smaller not-for-profit organizations have many of the same characteristics as owner-managed businesses, except in three key areas: the managers are not the owners, the boards are usually large and more interested in the objectives of the organization than in information security, and governance issues are highly important.

While this places a heightened responsibility on the management team to ensure that they are adequately in control of the information security aspects of their technology infrastructures, it shouldn't deter them from encouraging the board to form a small committee to oversee all information security and IT governance activity. The Finance Directors of smaller not-for-profits therefore need to include the broader IT governance issues in the overall remit of their departments.

6

Essentials for larger organizations

THREATS, VULNERABILITIES AND IMPACTS

The information security risks faced by larger organizations are of a different league from those faced by smaller ones. Both the threats and the vulnerabilities are significantly different and, as a result, larger organizations suffer more security incidents than the average: the 2004 ISBS, for instance, reported that 94 per cent of large companies had experienced an information security breach, compared with an overall rate of 74 per cent.

Threats

The threats, both external and internal, are more significant, and this reflects the perceived depth, quantity and value of the larger organization's information assets, its reputation and profile, and the number of people interested in targeting it. The 2004 ISBS showed that 91 per cent of larger organizations had suffered one or more malicious incidents, compared with an overall figure of only 68 per cent. Threats range from hackers through cyber-criminals, organized crime and activists of one sort or another to spies and cyber-terrorists – all depending on the organization.

Each sector has its own niche criminals: phishers target consumer financial services companies; industrial spies target intellectual property companies; activists target those companies they perceive as having an environmental or social impact of which they disapprove; hackers target those companies whose scalp will bring them the most prestige; and cyber-terrorists target those companies through which they think they can inflict the most damage. Fraudsters target any organizations where they can find a way of siphoning off cash, and probably work from inside.

More people are made redundant by, or fall out with, large organizations, and more contractors have their contracts terminated by large organizations – not proportionally, but in absolute terms, and simply because such large numbers of people are employed by any large organization. There are, therefore, likely to be many more people with a grudge against any one larger organization than there are against any smaller one.

Information leaked by a larger company is likely to be more price sensitive than that about a smaller one; details of its strategic plans (including mergers, acquisitions, restructurings, product launches, logistics, procurement, trial results, etc) are likely to have substantially more cash value than similar information from much smaller companies, and insiders are therefore more likely to be tempted to try to profit from such privileged information.

And, of course, for regulators and enforcers, targeting one or two non-compliant larger businesses brings a better return on investment than pursuing a number of smaller ones while, for institutional shareholders, the expectation is that larger organizations will be models of transparent, effective corporate governance and compliance.

Vulnerabilities

Paradoxically, larger organizations also, potentially, have more vulnerabilities than smaller ones. There are many reasons for this:

1. Almost all larger organizations have now gone digital: e-mail, employee internet access and transactional websites are standard; wireless networking and remote access are being rapidly deployed.
2. Larger organizations are more complex: they have multiple divisions and business units (each with its own management and operational ethos, each with sufficient local discretion to take actions that will seriously compromise the parent organization) operating internationally and across multiple jurisdictions, with different products and services and, therefore, different information technology needs.
3. Large organizations have often been built through a number of acquisitions, each of which brought a slightly different information technology infrastructure (architecture, hardware, operating systems, applications, bespoke software, working practices, culture, values and philosophy) to the party, not all of which has yet been (or is intended to be) successfully integrated into a single, harmonious whole.

4. While every system has its own vulnerabilities, the complexity of the whole creates another series of super-vulnerabilities. Most large organizations also have one or more legacy systems, which individual units or divisions may depend on, and which are no longer capable of integration into the overall architecture and may no longer be supported by their vendors. They work, though, for the moment.
5. Their multiple suppliers and volumes of customers all want electronic linkages with the company, and every such linkage is also a point of vulnerability.
6. Larger companies are more likely to have outsourced significant parts of their operations; every outsourcing contract is a potential vulnerability.
7. There are more people working in larger organizations; this means that there are more opportunities for someone to err, and for that error to have a negative impact on the availability, confidentiality or integrity of the organization's information assets. The 2004 ISBS, for instance, identified the fact that 42 per cent of large organizations had experienced an accidental systems failure and data corruption, compared with an overall rate of just 27 per cent.

Impacts

The impacts on larger businesses are significantly worse than they are as an overall average. According to ISBS 2004, percentages of large organizations, compared with the overall average, for each of the following, was:

- virus infection and software disruption: 68 per cent against 50 per cent;
- staff misuse of information systems: 64 per cent against 22 per cent;
- external intrusions into systems: 39 per cent against 17 per cent;
- computer-related theft or fraud: 49 per cent against 11 per cent.

The total cost of the worst incident, in a larger company, was between £65k and £190k, compared with a range of £7k to £14k overall. Information security is, for larger organizations, a much more serious undertaking than it is for smaller ones.

CHARACTERISTICS

Larger organizations are, in general, characterized by their complexity. They are likely to trade internationally and may have more than one stock exchange listing. They will certainly have a global customer and supplier base, and may have outsourced significant parts of their operations. They may have more than one consumer or business brand, and will almost certainly have a large product or service portfolio. They are also characterized by a process of almost continual change, as they respond to changes in their global marketplace. This creates a continuously changing mosaic of new vulnerabilities and unique challenges for information technology and for information security.

Multiple layers of management, many divisions, business units and operational entities, all translate into very complex network architectures. As the network map below indicates, a larger organization is likely to be complex, with multiple **protocols**, devices and activities; it may consist of a number of **LAN**s (Local Area Networks) connected within a **WAN** (**Wide Area Network**). The WAN might incorporate satellite stations as well as fixed-link fibre cables, and may or may not be outsourced, partially or in whole. Figure 6.1 shows an example of a multi-protocol network.

Executive management is usually more focused on strategic issues than day-to-day ones, and the executive management team is likely to be somewhat larger than in other organizations. Larger organizations are more likely to have a Chief Information Officer (CIO), who should (but does not always) have a seat on the board. In addition, there may be a CTO (Technology), a CSO (Security), a CISO (Information and Security) and a CCO (Compliance). Ideally, these roles would all be part of a single functional team that works closely with other functions. A considerable part of the directors' time will be taken up with governance issues, including shareholder relationships and related activity. The boards, which are increasingly supposed to have a preponderance of non-executive directors, have critical strategic and governance responsibilities.

IMPLEMENTATION ISSUES

Information security implementation in a large organization is almost always a governance issue. Information security is tightly linked into the requirements of the Combined Code and **Sarbanes Oxley**, as well as a myriad of other regulations and statutes with which directors have to ensure compliance.

The information security strategy has to support the business strategy, and has to reflect the fast-changing information technology infrastructure. That means that it has to be driven from the top, and it therefore needs to be addressed from the boardroom as part of an IT governance strategy. *IT Governance: Guidelines for Directors* addresses the top-level governance issues.

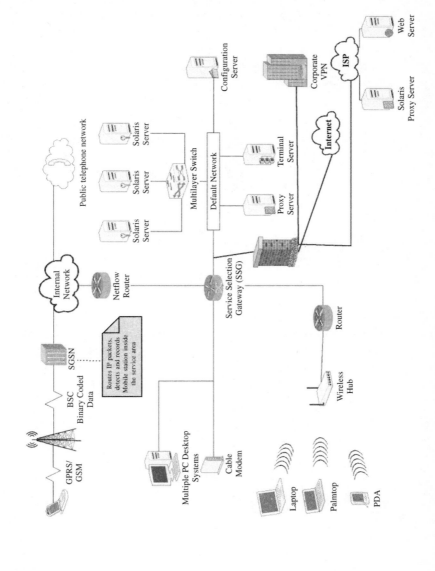

Figure 6.1 Complex, large, multi-protocol network

Scoping the information security project will be difficult. Unless it is a very uniform organization, it will be nearly impossible for the organization as a whole to try to implement a single ISMS. It is almost always better to break an organization-wide ISMS project down into a number of divisional or operating company-level projects and to provide a set of central resources and expertise (a corporate central support team) to coordinate activity and help take them forward. This central support unit should work closely with the central risk management function: information risk is just one of the risks that should be managed centrally.

Those organizations that have central security, legal and other support services will have to integrate them into the central information security support team; a major reason for information security project failure in large organizations is the vertical segregation of functions. Success does require a cross-organizational effort that is able to recognize, and respond to, blended threats. Ideally, each operating company will then be of a size to pursue the guidance given in Chapter 4 and, once the basics are securely in place, to raise the quality of the ISMS to at least the BS 7799/ISO 17799 level.

Each operational unit will almost certainly need to create a cross-functional project team, under the supervision of a director, to take the project forward. The detailed guidance of *IT Governance: A Manager's Guide to Data Security and BS 7799/ISO 17799* provides information on how to address the next stage. Effective, dedicated project management, for this project, will be as important as it is for any other large-scale IT project.

One of the key functions of the corporate central support team will be to determine the gateways between operational units and to resolve common issues that may affect architecture, protocols, contracting, procurement, conflicting security requirements, budgets, etc. It is important with this, as with any other major project, that the operational units are fully brought in, and committed to, the project: information security is as dependent on business culture as it is on technology.

The benefits of BS 7799/IS0 17799 certification are, for a large organization, very clear. The certificate is, firstly, external evidence that the organization has achieved – and is maintaining – an adequate level of information security management. Increasingly, this evidence will be demanded by clients, who want to be sure that their suppliers are secure. Secondly, the certificate is evidence, in a court or tribunal, that the board took appropriate and adequate steps to identify and comply with its various information security, data protection and privacy obligations, by implementing a system recognized as being a best-practice one. Thirdly, the need for ongoing compliance with the standard ensures that the organization continues to work at improving its Information Security Management System, which will mean it continues to respond to the changing, increasing range of information security threats.

UK PUBLIC SECTOR ORGANIZATIONS

The CSIA (Central Sponsor for Information Assurance) is the UK government's Cabinet Office unit, which is charged with working with the public and private sectors, and its international counterparts, to safeguard the United Kingdom's IT and telecommunications services. Specifically, the CSIA role is to provide a central, national focus for information security and its mission includes encouraging the private sector to develop a 'culture of security'. Its specific aims are to:

Provide a strategic direction for Information Assurance (IA) across the whole of the United Kingdom.

Coordinate and complement the activities of parties contributing to IA.

Sponsor activities that benefit the development of IA.

Accredit pan-government systems and in some cases such as the Government Secure Intranet, own the risk to shared information.

Identify and address vulnerabilities of national telecommunications systems and progress their resolution through a work programme, in conjunction with government departments or other involved organizations. (http://www.cabinetoffice.gov.uk/csia/)

Government departments and other organizations involved in the protection of the United Kingdom's critical information infrastructure (finance, telecommunications, utilities and emergency services, etc) include:

National Infrastructure Security Co-ordination Centre (NISCC);
National Hi-Tech Crime Unit (NHTCU);
Home Office;
Department of Trade and Industry;
Communications-Electronics Security Group (CESG);
The Cabinet Office.

All UK central government departments are required to meet internationally recognized information security management standards (for example, BS 7799) for their systems. The Cabinet Office's e-Government Interoperability Framework (e-GIF) defines the technical policies and specifications governing information flows across government and the public sector. The CSIA has also produced and maintains security framework documents that provide key guidance for both central and local government on providing secure online services, and these are available online from the publications section of the CSIA website.

The CSIA works with other government departments to maintain emergency telecommunications planning and business continuity plans. The CSIA works with business to address the vulnerabilities of public sector and commercial telecommunications systems as well as those of the financial and banking sector.

The public sector collects and holds substantial quantities of data on a daily basis. Some of it is extremely sensitive and personal, and the government is required to protect its confidentiality. Patient health records, social service details, tax returns – all are held on information systems. Private sector organizations also handle personal data and are required to comply with legislation governing the protection of that information.

Government departments are also subject to the Data Protection Act, the Human Rights Act and the Freedom of Information Act. This means that government information systems must protect the information they handle and make the correct information available when required, and only for use by those people who are authorized to have access to it. The Department for Constitutional Affairs has published guidance on *Data Sharing in the Public Sector* (see www.dca.gov.uk).

The UK central government has rolled out a secure intranet, the Government Secure Intranet (GSI), for its telecommunications and e-mail services and internet access. The GSI has been running since 1997. It imposes specific obligations on those organizations that wish to join it. It includes scope for local government and other government agencies to join, with the objective of 'creating a wider reaching, more secure and joined-up government service'.

The Cabinet Office requires central government departments to appoint a board-level Senior Information Risk Owner to be responsible for ensuring that departmental information security procedures are managed appropriately. This means that these procedures need to be based on (but not necessarily the same as – because there are specific central government versions of them) the controls of BS 7799.

The Office of the Deputy Prime Minister (ODPM) is encouraging local government to meet the same standards. Local authorities are obliged to comply with BS 7799 by 2005 as part of their *Implementing Electronic Government* (IEG) requirements. There is more information on electronic government on the ODPM website at www.localegov.gov.uk.

A key issue for public sector organizations is to find a balance between the bureaucracy of central government initiative implementation, the likelihood that the organizational board will not have on it any individuals with current or meaningful information security experience, and the fact that central government is an even more enticing target for the world's wrong doers.

7

Essentials for wireless networking

The deployment of wireless networking technology is growing even faster, in 2005, than the use of the internet. There are specific information security issues that need to be considered in respect of wireless networking, partly technological but primarily human: wireless networking frees individuals from the control of the centralized system administrator and enables them to work in ways that suit them, where, when and how it suits them. This is terrific for individuals, and is driving the dramatic increase in the deployment of the technology. It is also potentially a disaster, because individuals have always been the weakest link in any security system. This means that, for wireless networking to thrive, individual users have to make an individual, proactive effort to achieve at least the levels of security identified in this chapter and that all organizations need, not only to deploy the types of solution discussed here, but also to invest substantial effort in raising awareness and in training their employees.

WIRELESS NETWORKING

The explosive proliferation in laptops, PDAs (personal digital assistants), cellphones and wireless networks has given individuals greater flexibility, enabled organizations to be more responsive, driven down costs in a number of areas, and improved both productivity and competitiveness. Deploying a wireless network is quicker and substantially less expensive (or intrusive) than deploying traditional cabling.

It also brings a new range of vulnerabilities, not all of which are yet identified, and a growing range of threats. Of course, as wireless communication becomes an increasingly substantial part of the economic infrastructure, so it will become an increasingly interesting target for hackers, virus writers, cyber-criminals and the rest of the gangs.

Wireless networking is relatively easy: a child can set up a mobile phone or PDA out of the box, a first-time computer user can log onto a wireless **access point** using a modern laptop and anyone even minimally competent at basic DIY can set up a wireless network in as long as it takes to plug in a few wireless cards and run some simple software. There's nothing to it. And because there's nothing to it, you just get on with it, assuming that there are no vulnerabilities, threats or potentially serious impacts to worry about. But there *are*:

▓ Generally speaking, **WLAN**s (Wireless Local Area Networks) are so poorly set up that they are easier to hack into than fixed-link, cabled networks – but the information they carry is just as valuable as that on the more traditional cabled network.

▓ As an individual user of a wireless laptop – either in the home or using a public **HotSpot** – everything on your computer (everything) may be accessible to an outsider; and 'accessible' means, in this case, as easy as simply opening and reading any of your folders and files without your even being aware of it.

▓ An organization that deploys a WLAN is exposed – completely – by any 'rogue user' who brings an insecure wireless PC into the office (or, more terrifyingly, a branch office) and uses it to connect to the secure office network; the network is as vulnerable as its least secure point and the network security staff are unlikely even to be aware of a 'rogue user' – until it's much too late.

WIRELESS TECHNOLOGY

There are four wireless technologies to be aware of:

Bluetooth
infrared
mobile telephony
WiFi

Bluetooth

This is a short-range wireless technology. When two Bluetooth-enabled devices encounter one another, they can automatically communicate with each other to establish whether or not they should form a network, a PAN

(Personal Area Network). Bluetooth devices, particularly mobile phones, are at risk from two types of attack from nearby or passing devices, **bluejacking** and **bluesnarfing**. A bluejacking attack involves sending text messages to the mobile phones of any users who are within range, and it could be used both maliciously (for instance to hassle or bully someone) and for 'bluespam'. A bluesnarfing attack is potentially more serious, and involves the theft of all contact information stored in the phone. Some of this information could be particularly confidential and/or valuable to a third party. Not all phones are vulnerable and, as manufacturers respond to the discovery of these vulnerabilities, so there will be security improvements – and new exploits. The website, www.itgovernance.co.uk, links to a list of those mobile units currently said to be at risk. The only defence is to turn Bluetooth off, which is not very helpful. The other defence is to avoid buying any phones that are at risk of bluesnarfing and learn to live with the problems of bluejacking – after all, you simply need to move more than 10 metres away and, unless the perpetrator is following you, you will be out of range.

Infrared

Infrared (or **IrDA**) is a line-of-sight and one-to-one technology: this means it is effective only for uni-directional communication between devices that are within line-of-sight of each other. This means that there is no interference between communications and little problem in authentication of messages. These benefits are also limitations and infrared is not an effective communication method in other circumstances. The one risk associated with the technology is that it might provide a means by which the user of a secure device (for instance, a secure PDA) could transmit information to an unauthorized or non-secure device and, for this reason, some organizations with highly confidential information disable IrDA.

Mobile telephony

The mobile telephony universe has two originally distinct but now increasingly overlapping categories of devices: cellphones and PDAs. **Smart phones** are devices that have features of both categories and are, in this section, considered alongside PDAs, although the identified cellphone risks also apply.

Cellphones

There are a number of wireless telephony (cellphone) technologies, none of which we particularly need to examine in this book. Mobile telephony has long (apart from the unproved possibility that wireless radio waves might damage the brain) been considered very safe. The biggest information security risks relating to cellphones come from: a) the tendency of users to speak about confidential matters in public places – and, whether they do it at the top of their voices or in a loud whisper, there's a reasonable prospect that someone will hear what is said and will be able to make use of the information; and conversely, b) the fact that people can use cellphones to bypass security installed on corporate telephonic networks, whether call recording, call blocking or anything else. Cellphones (particularly privately owned ones) are the simplest and easiest way for someone in possession of confidential (financially sensitive) information to pass it beyond the organization's secure perimeter. This risk applies both to voice format information and to picture information – a phone photograph of a share price or a secret production process could have immediate value beyond the organization's secure perimeter.

Once these issues are dealt with – and it requires a combination of clearly stated policy, clearly written and understood employment contracts, straightforward staff training and an uncompromising disciplinary policy – then there is a small, but growing, number of cellphone security issues that also need to be considered. These risks are greater on smart phones, simply because of their greater functionality and the amount of data they carry and these are discussed as part of the coverage of PDAs, below. These other risks are, essentially, five:

▮ cellphone jammers;
▮ harassment, which was dealt with under Bluetooth, above;
▮ loss (through accident or theft) of essential data;
▮ tapping and hacking;
▮ viruses, worms, Trojans and malware.

Cellphone jammers can be purchased over the internet and can be fixed or mobile. Someone who simply wants to block other users can carry and operate a hidden jammer. While this is clearly a threat to the availability of data, it can be dealt with simply by moving away from the area of jamming; most jammers have a relatively short range.

Loss or compromise of data is a far greater issue. Millions of mobile phones are lost or stolen every year. When a phone is lost or stolen, two things happen, apart from the cost and inconvenience of the loss: someone else can use the phone to make telephone calls (which, from abroad, can make a painful hole in a mobile phone account) and the data (all the stored telephone numbers) on the telephone is lost to its owner.

There are four pretty obvious precautions that cellphone users should take:

1. Don't use the telephone in areas where it can be snatched, and keep an eye out for possible attackers.
2. Ensure that the telephone, when not in use, is secure – in a briefcase or handbag (itself kept within eyeshot) or in a pocket, but not just lying on the table where anyone who distracts your attention can grab it.
3. Back the telephone up – the phone should have been delivered with a CD ROM containing software that would enable you to keep a copy of the phone's contact data on your computer. You should run this backup routine on a regular basis – perhaps once per month. Then, if you lose your phone, it is relatively easy to reload the data onto a new phone – and it is equally easy to alert all your contacts that the phone has been stolen. This is particularly relevant for private telephone numbers of important people, whose privacy might have been compromised by your failure to safeguard your telephone. There might even, for some organizations, be potential data protection issues arising from such a failure.
4. Ensure that you pre-record (somewhere easily accessible – including for when you are abroad) the telephone's **IMEI** number and the emergency contact details of your network service provider so that, if the phone is lost or stolen, you can contact them and arrange for it to be blacklisted. Organizational internal helpdesks should record this information before issuing a telephone.

Tapping and hacking are more complex issues to deal with. While it has long been known that older analogue mobile phones can be hacked into, digital phones are a lot harder – but not impossible – to tap. The risk is that intentionally confidential conversations become potentially subject to eavesdropping and, possibly, **man in the middle** attacks. The only solutions currently available are to use the most recently available cellular phones (that is, those having the most current **encryption** methods), having first checked whether or not there is any evidence of their having been successfully hacked, or to acquire an ultra-secure cellphone that is capable of encrypting voice calls at 128-**bit** levels. SMS (Short Message Service) hacking, in which another user's SMS messages can be viewed, or spoofed SMS messages sent (sometimes in sufficient volumes to represent a denial of service (**DoS**) attack), are also emerging issues.

Mobile phone malware is an increasingly important issue. The possibility of spreading mobile phone viruses, worms and Trojans has been proven and only the relative simplicity of phones and their limited range of functions has prevented this from becoming more of an issue. **GPRS** and 3G networks, however, are likely to lead to an increase in the threat from viruses, hackers and malware of one sort or another. The practical counter measures at the time of writing this book were: to keep informed about the development of these threats and to take appropriate action as and when necessary; and to download, install and keep up to date a cellphone anti-virus software package.

Wireless PDAs and handheld computers

PDAs, handheld computers and smart phones are ubiquitous; they improve productivity and flexibility for individuals and employees. Almost everyone who has a PDA uses it for both personal and business purposes. Personal use includes storage of confidential personal data, including identity information, bank account details, user names, **PINs**, credit card details, etc. Business information includes confidential data about the employer, about clients, about suppliers, about problems and issues, a lot of which may also be subject to privacy or data protection legislation. There are therefore specific security risks, much greater than those related to ordinary cellphones, which need to be considered – not least because thieves and criminals all know how much confidential information is stored on PDAs and how poorly secured it is.

The risks that need to be considered for this type of device are not dissimilar to those that affect larger computers, particularly laptops, and are as follows:

- theft or loss of the device;
- viruses, Trojans, worms, other malware;
- theft of confidential information, including identity theft;
- denial of service attacks.

Theft or loss of a PDA or handheld computer is a significant security threat to individuals and a serious vulnerability for businesses and is a widespread problem. Anyone who has a PDA needs to take action. It might seem like a bit of a bore, but the moment that you lose a PDA is the moment that you realize how worthwhile it was to have followed the specific guidelines set out below: what you might almost call the Infosec Basics for PDAs.

Apart from the sensible practices that users can take to avoid having a PDA stolen or lost (which are pretty well the same as the basic practices identified above in relation to cellphones), the one practical step that might lead to the return of the PDA is to have the user's name and contact number in a visible location on the outside of the device – because, if all the information is protected, no one will be able to access anything, including your contact details. If the device carries confidential or classified information, you should install **bit-wiping software**.

The risk from viruses, Trojans, worms and other malware is zero – if the PDA is only ever operated in standalone mode. However, as half the benefit of the device comes from its wireless connectivity, it is vulnerable to malware. The risk is both to the PDA and to any computer or corporate network to which it connects, in that the malware could be transmitted. The only practical solution is to download, install and keep up to date appropriate anti-malware software. See www.itgovernance.co.uk for details on **airborne viruses** and software suppliers.

Theft of confidential information can be dealt with at two levels: the first is to password-protect files and data on the handheld; the second is to install encryption software that will ensure the data is secure. The website www.itgovernance.co.uk provides details about suppliers of encryption software for PDAs.

PDAs can connect to a corporate network using a secure **VPN (Virtual Private Network)**. They should. www.itgovernance.co.uk has information about suppliers of this software.

Enterprise deployment of PDAs

Some organizations issue PDAs to their employees. A far greater number of organizations don't; their employees nevertheless use their own and will synchronize them with their corporate desktop computers. Organizations should take proactive steps to deal with this through the development and deployment of specific PDA-related policies and guidelines that prohibit employees from connecting either corporate or personal PDAs to corporate equipment unless corporate requirements have been met. These requirements (which should be written into any employee user agreement) are extensions to the Infosec Basics for Business, should be proportionate to the actual risks (using a risk assessment) that the organization faces, and might include the following:

- PDAs must be password-protected, preferably with a strong password or two factor authentication (rule 7).
- The wireless port on PDAs must be disabled (to prevent transmission of confidential data to unauthorized individuals) (rule 7) and wireless **cloaking bags** must be used.
- PDAs must not be left unattended on desks (while charging, for instance) (rule 5) – unless, possibly, it is secured in a locked device or has an appropriate alarm.

- Appropriate anti-malware software must be installed and kept up to date (rule 6).
- A PDA-level firewall should be installed (rule 8).
- PDA operating systems must have the latest patches installed (rule 9).
- Depending on the corporate risk assessment, wireless connection to the corporate network could be restricted to a secure VPN or using **GSM** (Global System for Mobile Communications) or GPRS technology (Blackberries, for instance) (rule 8).
- Any confidential corporate information stored on a PDA must be encrypted (rules 3 and 7), perhaps stored in an encrypted database.
- Possibly, PDAs carrying highly confidential information should have automatic bit-wiping software installed.
- Back up regularly – by synchronizing with the linked computer (rule 11).

WiFi

WiFi is the name given to the **802.11** (see under E in glossary) family of wireless standards and, by extension, to any equipment that is designed to their specification. 802.11 equipment is only compatible within the 802.11 family if it has been designed that way and, if it has, it will usually be **WiFi certified**.

WiFi equipment is usually sold and installed with its default security settings. These settings are 'no security'. That's: NO SECURITY. 'No security' means that anyone, including the completely innocent, can connect to the wireless computer or wireless network and use it for their own communication purposes, to access shared resources on the network, and even to access individual folders and files. A malicious user could use an unsecured wireless computer or network for spam, for malware releases, for cyber-crime or cyber-terrorism purposes. This activity can then be traced back to the unsecured wireless access point and therefore to the individual or business that owns and operates the access point.

WiFi networks are extremely vulnerable, because it is not possible to implement the sort of physical perimeter that prohibits third parties from joining a fixed-link network. It is therefore essential that **networks** and individual computers are properly secured against logical access by anyone within range who has **war driving** equipment.

RISKS

There are seven risks specifically associated with WLANs:

1. Insertion attacks, where an unauthorized device (laptop or PDA), or an additional, rogue **AP** (access point) is connected to the network.
2. Interception and monitoring of network traffic or wireless communications, enabling capture of user names, passwords and other sensitive data. The **evil twin** is a particularly nasty version of this attack.
3. Jamming, either inadvertently by other devices (cordless phones, baby monitors, other **802.11b/g** devices etc) using the 2.4 **GHz** band, or deliberately by attackers who deploy tools to overwhelm the frequency so as to deny service to legitimate users.
4. Client-to-client attacks, in which one device bypasses the AP to attack another device, either to attack file sharing or with a denial of service attack.
5. **Brute force attacks** to establish the AP passwords – made much simpler, of course, if the widely known default passwords for each device have not been changed.
6. Encryption attacks, to break the encryption code and access the encrypted information, are particularly easy on WLANs that either have no encryption or only **WEP** (Wired Equivalent Privacy)-compliant. Even **WPA** (WiFi Protected Access) is not immune to a hacker.
7. Configuration attacks are made possible by the fact that wireless devices ship with no security in order to make deployment speedy and easy. As a result, the basic configuration of APs are widely known and, as it is very easy for a war driver or hacker to establish the manufacturer of the AP, it is just as easy to access the AP and change its configuration – maliciously.

Basics

The biggest risk associated with WiFi activity is, in fact, the loss or theft of the WiFi-enabled laptop. Before taking any action to secure WiFi communication, it is important to establish the physical security of the device itself. The risks associated with the physical loss of a laptop include (but are not limited to):

■ loss of confidential or proprietary information, which might expose the organization to loss of competitiveness, loss of reputation, loss of clients, loss of suppliers, compromise of business operations or of individuals, breach of stock exchange regulations affecting confidential information exposure, etc;

▓   loss of private information, which might expose the organization to breach of privacy and data protection legislation;

▓   loss of irreplaceable information, which might expose the organization to severe disruption;

▓   loss of confidential access information (user names, passwords), which might enable a malicious acquirer of the laptop to access and compromise (or plunder) organizational resources;

▓   loss of a network authenticated device, which might be used maliciously for accessing secure organizational facilities.

So, the physical security issues are paramount. In the office, physical security means the use of locking cables during the day, to ensure that laptops that are in use on desks are not simply picked up and removed. At night, it means securing laptops in a purpose-built laptop safe or the removal of the laptop from the premises by its user.

Laptop physical security is, outside the office, more complex. In theory, laptops are safer at home (if home is occupied) than they are in an unattended office and that is probably true – as long as they don't contain highly confidential information, in which case alternative protective measures need to be taken. No, the real problem is in transit: it's what happens to the laptop in the coffee shop, in its bag on the bus or train, or in the cab. More laptops are lost in cabs than by any other means. The basic guidance (apart from paying attention) is, firstly, to store laptops in nondescript carry bags, or inside briefcases, anything that doesn't look like a computer case, so as not to encourage a passing criminal to consider stealing it. Secondly, keep a firm hold on the laptop in its case at all times, especially in bars, hotels and while using public transport. Thirdly, do not leave a laptop unattended, not in a public place, not on view inside a vehicle, not anywhere. But everyone knows this – the important thing is to DO IT!

Thereafter, the basics must be applied. For businesses, the Infosec Basics for Business must apply in WLANs and, for SoHo users, the Internet Highway Code is as applicable for wireless use as it is for fixed-line use. As a minimum, any wireless computer must have appropriate password protection, its own firewall and anti-malware software. Additional steps are required to ensure that the wireless infrastructure is adequately secured.

The keys to wireless security are encryption and authentication. A secure WLAN will have addressed both.

Encryption

Two types of encryption are available for 802.11 WLANs: WEP and WPA. WEP has a number of well-known holes in it. It is better than nothing, but wireless equipment is delivered without even being WEP-enabled. If your hardware supports both types of encryption, you should apply WPA. If it only supports WEP, and if two WEP keys are available, choose the 104-bit key. If only the 40-bit key is available, go for that. Above all, enable encryption on the laptop and on the AP. Computers running Windows XP with SP2 installed support WPA. This is (another) good reason to upgrade to XP SP2.

Authentication

802.11 WLANs use one of four methods of authentication: open system, shared key, **802.1X** and WPA with a pre-shared key.

Open system authentication works in **infrastructure mode**, but is ultra-crackable. It doesn't work in **ad hoc** configurations. Wireless networking AP equipment is usually not even set up for open system authentication. Authentication inside a business should be based on the 802.1X standard, using a **domain controller** and a **RADIUS** (Remote Authentication Dial-In User Service) server, following the recommendations in *Enterprise Deployment of Secure 802.11 Networks Using Microsoft Windows* at: http://www.microsoft.com/technet/prodtechnol/winxppro/deploy/default.mspx

RECOMMENDED ACTIONS

Businesses and individuals should upgrade to WPA as soon as possible and be alert for future upgrade options as they become available. It is an all-or-nothing option: either everything on the WLAN is WPA-enabled or nothing is. This means that, in a SoHo network, every wireless device (including routers, printers, game stations, screens, etc) must be upgraded to WPA and must support Windows Connect Now, a feature that automates WLAN configuration. The first step, therefore, is to establish if upgrades are available (as downloads, from the websites of the manufacturer) for each device connected to the WLAN. If not, you will have to replace the product(s) with newer, WPA-enabled equipment. The **WiFi Alliance** website provides details of products that it has certified as having met the WPA standard and which are therefore interoperable. If it is not possible to upgrade all the hardware that uses the WLAN to WPA, it will unfortunately be necessary to stick with WEP and all the risks associated with it.

Windows XP SP2 supports WPA, which means that any computer using that as an operating system (OS) will be ready for a WPA-enabled WLAN. See the directions above regarding older OSs.

Once upgrades or replacements have been identified for each device on the WLAN, deploy them. Start by upgrading the router or other wireless AP and then upgrade all the other devices that will run on the WLAN. Once all the devices are capable of supporting WPA, it is very easy to set up a secure wireless network.

Automated WPA wireless network configuration

In Windows XP SP2, the Wireless Network Setup Wizard guides the user through all the steps necessary to configure a secure network. This methodology is adequate for both a small enterprise deployment (although large-scale deployment of WPA-Enterprise uses the 802.1X authentication framework and verifies network users through a separate authentication server) and for a SoHo network. A USB **flash** stick is also required. The wizard can be run on any computer that will access the WLAN and it will create settings that it will write to the USB flash stick for transfer to every other device that is required to access the WLAN. Full, step-by-step instructions are available at: http://www.microsoft.com/technet/community/columns/cableguy/cg0604.mspx, but the wizard is very straightforward. The key choices to be made during the process are:

1. to choose and assign a network name, or **SSID** (Service Set Identifier), that will not obviously identify the physical location of the AP to a war driver;
2. choose *Use WPA Encryption*;
3. choose *Use a USB flash drive*.

After that, simply follow the instructions, inserting the USB flash stick into each of the devices (starting with the wireless AP) so that they can automatically be configured to match the initial configuration and connect to the WLAN.

Manual WPA wireless network configuration

There are a number of situations in which it may be necessary to manually configure the network. Using the Windows XP SP2 Wireless Network

Setup Wizard, there is a prompt to print out the wireless network settings so that they can be programmed into each device manually.

If your computer infrastructure is such that it is not possible to configure a wireless network using the Microsoft Wizard, you are likely to need specialist assistance. However you do it, it is important that you take the necessary action to secure your WLAN.

Enterprise wireless network configuration

Even a WPA-enabled WLAN poses a security risk to organizations. WPA, while more secure than WEP, is still capable of being cracked. The logical way to deal with this is to place a firewall between the AP (with the AP itself protected by a firewall) and the fixed network, so that any access attempts to the network can be controlled at that gateway, in line with the corporate access policy.

The second area of risk is from a 'rogue user' inside the corporate network perimeter who plugs a portable AP into an available network device and who then accesses the network from a computer that doesn't even have WEP enabled. There are two obvious risks: the first is that the 'rogue user' might be malicious and could use this wireless access maliciously; the second is that, while the 'rogue user' might not be malicious, someone else might be and, given the absence of any security on the 'rogue user's' computer, might choose to access the network for their own purposes. No firewalls can prevent this scenario; organizations need (depending on a risk assessment) to either authenticate and encrypt all communications within the firewalled corporate network (not an inexpensive option) or to deploy a network monitoring tool that will identify unauthorized wireless APs.

In fact, organizations need to extend the Infosec Basics for Business to cover WLANs. All the basic rules must be extended to specifically cover wireless networking. For instance:

- A wireless security policy (rule 1) should clearly define how the organization intends to deal with these risks.
- All APs should be treated as **untrusted** (rule 9).
- All APs should be subject (rule 8) to appropriate security architecture (defined configuration requirements, DMZ (demilitarized zone), etc).
- All APs and clients should undergo monitoring (rule 12) and assessment (regular security audits and penetration tests to ensure they are not compromised).
- Network surveillance (also rule 12) should be considered (searching for rogue APs or communications in the air between a wireless client and an AP).

- ▓ Install appropriate protection for wireless clients (including anti-malware (rule 6) as well as laptop-level firewalls (rule 8).
- ▓ Specific training (rule 14) for WLAN users is essential, as is proper documentation of user access rights (rule 7) and of all related procedures (rule 13).
- ▓ All wireless devices must be securely linked into the corporate update, upgrade and patch program (rule 9).

WiFi security on the road

While an increasing number of public HotSpots are deploying WPA connection software, many others (including those set up in corporations for visitors) are still open. In other words, they are configured with no or minimal security, in order to encourage users. WPA will probably be set to 'off'. Any user who connects to a HotSpot is probably operating unsecured on an unsecured network. You should assume that any of the seven risks associated with WLANs and which were identified earlier in this chapter could apply to you. Clearly, wherever possible, a WPA service should be used, even though there is a cost implication. (Most mobile phone providers offer secure HotSpot technology.) There are (apart from the basics, particularly the laptop-level firewall) some essential safety precautions you should take if you are using an open HotSpot:

- ▓ If possible, designate the HotSpot network as an *untrusted* or *internet* zone network in your firewall settings – the firewall may be able to detect that the network is a HotSpot one and make these changes automatically.
- ▓ Turn off file and printer sharing – otherwise anyone else using the HotSpot or with a wireless device in the vicinity could access data on your computer.
- ▓ Any folders containing confidential or sensitive information on your laptop should already be (strong) password-protected.
- ▓ Use a VPN for communicating any confidential information with your organization.
- ▓ Be careful about what else you do and what information you key in – for instance, ensure that any confidential information (for example, credit card details) only gets entered into a site that uses SSL (Secure Sockets Layer) technology.
- ▓ Encrypt any e-mail (through the *Options* button in the Outlook e-mail toolbar, where you can set the security at the individual message level quickly and easily) that you want to keep confidential.

TELEWORKING

Organizations and individuals both need to think through all the security issues that are peculiar to teleworkers. Teleworking has become, increasingly, an extension of mobile working, rather than being simply one or a few workers based outside the organizational perimeter and accessing the network from time to time. The only significant difference between mobile working and teleworking is that teleworking involves a fixed base and fixed connection to the organizational network, as a result of which, there is more corporate information – and equipment – in the teleworking employee's home. The home, of course, does not have anything like the physical security that might be available in the work place and is also vulnerable to domestic thieves and incidents.

In considering the options around teleworking, both the employee and the employer should consider carefully all the issues before going ahead, as it is probably easier not to start than it is to unwind if it goes wrong. The most important decision regards the equipment that is to be used. If the employer is deploying all the equipment, then it is perfectly reasonable to insist that the employee observes all (ALL) the computer-related policies and procedures required of office-based staff.

If, however, the employee is using their own equipment for corporate work, then the decisions are a bit harder. The key objectives, from the employer's point of view, are that any confidential information that is in the employee's house (whether digital or on paper) should be secure, and that the employee's access to the corporate network does not create a vulnerability. To this end, the employer needs to be clear about the security requirements and, if necessary, to provide the additional software and hardware (documented as being on a loan basis), plus the training, to ensure that security is achieved and maintained. Other issues that will need to be addressed in these circumstances include:

- Who should own business ideas or intellectual property developed on privately owned equipment either during or after working hours?
- How are disputes to be resolved?
- How is the organization to access the equipment (either to check security or as part of an investigation)?
- What will be the effect on software licensing agreements consequent upon the deployment to a private machine of organization-specific software?

A key issue to consider is the physical security of the site. Look at the physical security of the proposed building (usually a house) and also take into account the security of the surrounding area. The teleworking environment within the building should also be assessed: is it a separate office or is it in a communal area? The communications requirement should be particularly carefully assessed, taking into account the type of technology (telephone, fax machine, computer, printer, scanner, internal modem, ISDN, ADSL, etc) that may be required, where and how it will be fitted, how it will be removed on termination, and who bears the costs of which bits of the operation. The threat of unauthorized access to the facilities (including from family and friends) should also be assessed and, while health and safety issues are specifically beyond the scope of this book, both employee and employer should take adequate steps to ensure that all the provisions of all the regulations covering health and safety are fully met.

Key decisions, which reflect both the Infosec Basics for Business and the Internet Highway Code, must be taken by employee and employer together. A large employer is likely to dictate these as a matter of policy, and require an employee to sign a teleworker user agreement that reflects these policies. A smaller employer may need to agree these individually with each teleworker and then document them in a user agreement. Either way, there will need to be adequate training to ensure that the teleworker is able to meet the agreed requirements. The key decisions are:

1. Physical security, ensuring that the equipment is to be protected against breakage and theft, and that there is appropriate insurance cover (it should not be left to the employee to organize cover under a household policy, as this will usually not be applicable).
2. The teleworker should comply with the organization's requirements about passwords and screensavers. There should be very clear rules about what access families and friends can have to the corporate facilities and to the company's equipment. Critically, this must take into account any other devices that may run on a home network and any wireless devices or wireless networking.
3. Automatic patch updating should be required, and the organization should deploy technology that will not allow a home computer to log onto the corporate network unless it is up to date with its patching.
4. There must be a personal firewall on the remote computer.
5. There must be up-to-date anti-virus software and the organization should deploy technology that will not allow a home computer to log onto the network unless its anti-virus software is up to date.
6. Spam filtering should be deployed to protect remote computers.
7. Teleworkers should be required to deploy the same anti-malware tools as the rest of the organization and to keep them updated and active.
8. Teleworkers must be trained, so they know what to look out for, what they may do and what they may not do.

9. There should be clear rules about backup and business continuity plans, with appropriate resources provided. It should be borne in mind that the risks to the organization are greater in relation to individual teleworkers than in relation to individual users in the corporate office environment. Teleworkers should certainly be subject to audit and monitoring just as is any other person on the network, and there should also be a documented process for revoking general or specific teleworking authorization and to ensure that equipment is all returned on termination.

10. Appropriate steps should be taken to provide hardware and software support and maintenance; most usually, this includes an extended service from the organizational help-desk, whose hours will need to be extended to cover teleworking and whose skills will need to encompass their peculiar problems.

8

Essentials for e-commerce

The e-commerce world is changing rapidly, and e-commerce is becoming a fact of life for most businesses and individuals. This has immediate and constantly changing implications for information security. Organizations are changing, becoming more open; they are also becoming more complex. As companies acquire others, or develop business partnerships, so they want to share information across spaces that are no longer strictly limited to an organizational domain. The drive toward more open business models is driving forward greater interconnection and greater sharing of information.

Technology is contributing to these changes, as more and more powerful applications are developed to push information around the world and to overcome any barriers in its way. Content is no longer limited to text; it now includes documents and active content (mobile code, such as **Java** or **ActiveX**) that download and run on users' desktops; it includes voice, sound, animation, streaming video, instant messaging, file transfers and a whole range of multimedia applications. All these changes help the development of e-commerce, so both organizations and users want to respond to and use all the new capabilities; this also creates a whole new and fast-changing series of risks and vulnerabilities and a very porous organizational security perimeter.

THREATS AND VULNERABILITIES

Technology changes are at the heart of these changing threats. Applications are increasingly written to assume that information will be shared across networks, regardless of the organizational boundaries or firewalls between them. Many vendors are now actually building their applications to overcome or circumvent the firewall controls, which are often viewed as barriers to e-commerce and which are to be overcome in the pursuit of an open, networked world.

One ongoing change is that increasing numbers of internet application developers are making new applications run via the firewall port that is most commonly open (port 80, traditionally enabled on 99.9 per cent of firewalls to run **HTTP** (Hypertext Transfer Protocol). This means that a diversity of media types try to navigate port 80, making it difficult for firewalls to filter out malware or to control access to specific data channels. Of course, as new applications are developed and firewalls lag behind in their ability to effectively handle them, so organizations will take increasing risks by opening their firewalls anyway – particularly where the application is considered critical to the business.

The risk from hackers is growing all the time. Organized crime, as was described in Chapter 1, is turning to the internet and e-commerce as a lucrative business area and the growth of phishing attacks and spam are two of the most visible and high-profile indicators of the extent to which e-commerce is also a danger area for consumers and businesses. Equally important are the risks arising from industrial espionage and the value that transactional information can have to a competitor, even if it has only been inadvertently disclosed.

E-commerce issues can be divided into three categories: those that relate to the information published on the website, those that relate to the security of the commercial transaction and those that relate to the security of the website itself.

INFORMATION PUBLICATION

Electronically published information (for example, on a web server accessible via the internet) will need to comply with legislation and probably with legislation in the country in whose jurisdiction the web server is hosted and the country in whose jurisdiction the transaction takes place. This is still a grey area, particularly for organizations that supply their products and services internationally across the web, and specialist legal advice should be taken on what rules, regulations and laws should be observed, and where and how.

It is possible, for instance, that an organization might decide that the risk of prosecution in a number of jurisdictions is such that it will take particular steps to comply with local laws, or that it will not allow people from those jurisdictions to use their websites. It is important that the organization does decide what controls it needs to put into place to protect the information that it publishes.

Electronic publishing systems (that is, websites) that permit users to provide feedback or to otherwise enter data, particularly while carrying out a transaction, should have a number of controls. These should include the following:

- Any information that is to be published on the website should be approved in advance by someone appropriately experienced, against a pre-set checklist, that ensures that whatever is published falls within the organization's commercial, marketing and legal criteria. It is particularly important to remember that publishing information electronically may have the same consequences as publishing it any other way. People may rely on it, and the laws covering libel will also apply! As it is published to the world, it is possible that the potential liability may depend on the jurisdiction where the information is read and relied on. It is certainly wise, particularly for websites that publish information from more than one supplier (or which have links to other sites, or act as portals, aggregating information from a number of organizations), for there to be a **disclaimer** making clear what material emanates from the publisher and what from other sources. This disclaimer should make it clear that the publisher accepts no responsibility for third-party material.
- Any information that is obtained from people using the website should be done so in accordance with data protection legislation; for UK companies this means compliance with the Data Protection Act. Specific consideration should be given to the legal issues that arise when a UK registered company collects and stores personal data on a web server that is geographically located outside the United Kingdom.
- Information input into the site should be processed quickly, accurately and properly so that a third party does not have time to access it and so that the records stored are correct. This applies particularly to individual personal and financial data, and to corporate commercial information entered onto an extranet.

TRANSACTIONAL SECURITY

Non-repudiation is a major issue for e-commerce. As commercial transactions take place over the internet, the same types of dispute that arise in the analogue world arise in the digital one. Disputes can involve the specifics of agreements and performance and there are digital equivalents of the postmarks, recorded delivery receipts and notarized documents that exist in the analogue world. There are three key components to non-repudiation:

▨ Non-repudiation of origin. There must be evidence for a receiving party that the sender is genuine, not an impostor. A vendor would, for instance, want to be sure that an order was from a genuine customer.

▨ Non-repudiation of submission. There must be evidence that the thing was actually sent at a particular time (such as a postmark).

▨ Non-repudiation of receipt. It must be possible to prove that the receiving party has actually received what was sent. Lesser issues include verifying the time and place of transmission.

Many, but not all, of the issues listed above can be solved by implementing effective cryptographic controls, which may require input from a vendor of appropriate technology. Organizations need to deploy appropriate controls that have been developed to deal specifically with e-commerce transactions, and they should be incorporated into a trading agreement between online **b2b** (business to business) trading partners. Trading partners operating through an internet exchange or via an extranet also need to resolve these issues.

These controls need to be extended to cover business to consumer (**b2c**) commerce for all those organizations selling across the web, particularly in respect of the implications of the Data Protection Act, phishing attacks and credit card fraud. Any e-commerce organization also needs to tackle key issues of jurisdiction, to establish which country's laws will cover its transactions, and for this it will need to take specific legal advice.

You must ensure that your website carries a statement of your privacy policy (which must, of course, comply with the legislation in your local jurisdiction) and it must carry your Terms of Business. You need professional legal advice, from an internet-aware lawyer, on both these documents.

WEBSITE SECURITY

E-commerce organizations will adopt one of two strategies in respect of their e-commerce site functionality: they will either own (and be responsible for) their server **platform**, or they will contract with an organization that supplies that service, who usually also provides some form of web retailer package that can be integrated with their website and with an Online Payment Service. The security issues in each case are different: if the servers are owned in-house, security has to be tackled in-house; if the website is outsourced, then the quality of the provider's security is the issue.

Organizations need to take specific steps to protect ('harden') their web servers from attack. There are a number of baseline security measures that should be documented. The starting point, if the organization is running its web servers in-house, is to apply the **CIS** benchmarks to their configuration. These can be downloaded from www.cisecurity.org and they run through a downloadable Security Scoring Tool and can be managed by the system administrator. Ensuring that servers are configured and patched to at least these standards should be a minimum requirement. You can also purchase step-by-step guides from **SANS** for a number of systems. It is possible that, following a risk assessment, you might decide that the site needs further security upgrading, but that requires input from a professional information security adviser and is beyond the scope of this book.

Web servers should be set up in a DMZ (demilitarized zone), themselves protected by appropriate firewalls and routers. Backup and business continuity issues will need proper consideration.

Web applications must filter user-supplied data. Raw user input could contain all sorts of things that the organization does not want on its system. Hackers can access corporate networks through websites. The application must therefore enforce the content type of data entered so that, for instance, a numerical input can only be a number and all non-numeric characters must be filtered to exclude string and query terminators, wildcard selectors and all sorts of other unusual input. Specialist advice should be sought to ensure that the most current technological defences have been incorporated into the application.

If the website is outsourced, you should find out from your provider what their approach to securing their web servers is. You should ask about the server environment, (the servers should be in a **server farm**) the standards to which the servers are configured, and check whether or not the organization is certificated to BS 7799/IS0 17799. You should also ask for evidence about what security incidents they have handled in the last nine months, and how much downtime their clients suffered. You should ask for references (preferably, substantial organizations who have been clients for at least a year), and you should check with them as to the security record.

You will want to be sure that the way personal data is collected and where it is held will enable you to comply with Data Protection Act and privacy rules – see www.itgovernance.co.uk for current information on these issues. You will also want to ensure that integration with your Online Payment Provider is effective, and that payment details are properly protected.

9

Legal and regulatory essentials

INTRODUCTION

All organizations, businesses and individuals working with information and operating one or more computers is subject to – or protected by – a wide range of information and computer-specific legislation and regulation. This chapter outlines the key legislation and regulations that should be considered, but is not intended to be an authoritative guide. Current legal advice must be taken from qualified, specialist legal advisers if an individual or organization wants or needs to rely on any matter discussed here. This chapter deals with current compliance issues for organizations based or operating in or supplying the UK market, and identifies relevant US legislation that may affect UK-based businesses. Laws are likely to be different in other countries and, therefore, organizations based elsewhere should take specialist local advice.

Organizations based in the United Kingdom with operations elsewhere in the world will need to deal with the UK requirements as well as those of the foreign countries in which they operate and, again, specialist legal advice should be taken. This chapter also does not deal with governance requirements (the UK's Combined Code, the Turnbull Guidance, the OECD principles or Sarbanes Oxley) as these are substantially covered in *IT Governance: A Manager's Guide to Data Security and BS 7799/ISO 17799*.

Web trading (even if the organization is based in the United Kingdom) could potentially take place in a multitude of countries and the law in this area is constantly changing and developing. Any organization that is trading across the web without limits on who may access its website should take specialist advice to ensure that contractual and trading terms are watertight and that issues of jurisdiction and which law (that of the country in which the server is based, or the organization is based, or the customer is based, or to which delivery is made) will apply to any transaction, have been resolved, and to ensure that there is an appropriate acceptance and/or waiver of liability on the entrance to the website.

Foreign legislation may also be applicable to the operations of the organization; in particular, legislation passed in the United States (such as the **Digital Millennium Copyright Act** and others, discussed below) may impact the international operations of UK-based organizations or may be the basis on which a US-based organization takes action against a UK-based one. Again, expert legal advice is necessary and the rapid, ongoing development of the law should be tracked on a regular basis, through newsletters such as Herbert Smith's IT e-bulletin (subscribe at www.herbertsmith.com).

The legislation that any organization might need to consider could include, but is not necessarily limited to, the following.

EU regulation

EU Directives have been, and will continue to be, significant drivers of UK regulation. The two most important EU instruments are the EU Data Protection Directive of 1995 (note that although the United States was declared a **'safe harbour'** for the purposes of EU data protection regimes in 2000 only a relatively small number of US companies fall within the 'safe harbour') and the EU Privacy Directive of 2003. These directives give the context for the UK legislation, identified and discussed below, and for any changes that may occur in future.

UK legislation

Intellectual property rights ('IPR'), through the Copyright Designs and Patents Act 1988 (the 'CDPA'), is one of the most obvious legal issues for most information processing systems, but there is a web of other, relevant legislation. One of the most important of these is the Data Protection Act 1998 ('the DPA') and, in addition to this, there is the Human Rights Act 1998 (the 'HRA'), the Regulation of Investigatory Powers Act 2000 (the 'RIPA'), the Computer Misuse Act 1990, the Electronic Communications Act 2000 and the Privacy and Electronic Communications Regulations 2003. The Freedom of Information Act (the 'FOIA') was passed in 2000 and, while primarily applicable to public bodies, it has the potential to force confidential commercial information about (for instance) public sector contracts into the public arena.

In the United Kingdom there is a complex array of anti-money laundering laws including the Terrorism Act 2000, the Proceeds of Crime Act 2002 and the Money Laundering Regulations 2003; these laws do not only affect banks and financial institutions and every organization's trade body should be able to identify whether or not their sector is affected and whether or not detailed client verification records will need to be maintained and kept secure.

There is an increasing amount of corporate governance legislation being passed in the United Kingdom, which will require the collection and storage of commercially sensitive data in order to satisfy reporting obligations. In order to comply, directors will need to satisfy themselves that the IT system itself does not pose any operational risks to the company. These requirements are contained in general legislation such as the Companies (Audit, Investigations and Community Enterprise) Act 2004 as well as in sector-specific regulation enforced by bodies such as the Financial Services Authority.

US legislation

Relevant US legislation and regulation includes the Gramm-Leach-Bliley Act (the 'GLBA'), dealing with consumer financial data; the Fair Credit Reporting Act (the 'FRCA'), designed to protect people from identify theft; the Health Insurance Portability and Accountability Act (the 'HIPAA'), which requires healthcare organizations to protect – and keep up to date – their patients' healthcare records; the SEC's regulation FD, which bars selective disclosure of material non-public information; the SEC's rule 17 a-4, which requires broker dealers to retain trading records (therefore including e-mails, etc) for six years; section 404 of Sarbanes Oxley (the overall importance of which is much greater than this single issue), which requires companies to safeguard (amongst other assets) their information, including e-mails, attachments, etc; the Californian Senate Bill 1386, which requires notification of breaches of personal data security; and the California Online Privacy Protection Act of 2004 (the 'OPPA'), which requires websites serving Californians (irrespective of their geographic or jurisdictional location) to comply with strict privacy guidelines.

Other regulations

The Bank of International Settlements (BIS) through the Basel 2 accord has laid down very clear guidelines for banks and financial institutions worldwide, including the requirement that (by 2007) three years of operational data needs to have been recorded and retained.

Of course, the huge growth in Anti-Money Laundering regulation, including the requirements of the international Joint Task Force and the USA PATRIOT Act broaden the requirement on organizations to verify client details and, therefore, to keep those personal details secure and in line with applicable data security regulations.

DATA PROTECTION ACT 1998 (THE 'DPA')

The DPA requires any organization that processes personal data to comply with eight enforceable principles of what it identifies as good practice. The eight principles are that personal data must be:

▓ fairly and lawfully processed;
▓ processed for the specified purposes;
▓ adequate, relevant and not excessive;
▓ accurate and up to date;
▓ kept no longer than necessary;
▓ processed in accordance with the data subject's rights;
▓ secure – which means technical and organizational security;
▓ not transferred to countries that do not provide adequate protection for the data.

The DPA (which is interpreted in the light of the Human Rights Act 2000) is concerned with personal data, and this encompasses facts and opinions about an individual and includes information about the Data Controller's intentions toward the individual (for example, will s/he be employed or not?). Under the terms of the DPA, 'processing' includes storage, and the requirements apply to both electronic data and paper records (if they are contained in a 'relevant filing system'). The precise definitions of what is, and is not, covered have been further complicated by the findings of the 2003 *Durant* v. *Financial Services Authority* court case and the Information Commissioner's updated guidance (on his website) must be taken into account.

Any organization that is going to process personal data (a Data Controller) must register with the Information Commissioner (this is called notification) and the register entry will include the name and address of the Data Controller together with a general description of what personal data are processed. Notification (and changes to notification details) can be completed online at www.informationcommissioner.gov.uk. Failure to notify is a strict liability offence. Individuals can consult the register to establish what Data Controllers have notified to the Commissioner, and the register can be searched online. Notification lasts one year and must then be renewed. The site address shown above will also provide substantially more information about the DPA, including details of current notification and renewal fees.

The Information Commissioner is the only statutory authority in the United Kingdom for administering and maintaining the public register of Data Controllers. Communication from any other organization claiming to be a data protection notification agency is likely to be part of an attempted fraud as the agency is almost certainly bogus. The Information Commissioner and the Office of Fair Trading are, at any one time, dealing with a number of such bogus agencies, and full details of these agencies and their activities can also be found on the Information Commissioner's website.

The DPA covers a number of areas, including CCTV records, websites and internet activity, recruitment and selection of staff, employment records, staff monitoring (including, for example, checking telephone records or internet use) and information about workers' health.

The Information Commissioner's website provides detailed guidance and a number of specific codes of practice (some general codes and others specific to the public or private sectors), on the steps necessary for an organization to comply with the DPA. In this guidance, he describes the approach that an organization should follow in its effort to comply with the seventh principle of the DPA. This approach is in line with BS 7799, to which he refers readers for further advice. It would be fair to assume, from this, that implementation and certification of an ISMS would be regarded as an appropriate step to comply with the requirements of the seventh principle of the DPA.

The key point is that Data Controllers must comply with the DPA; failure to do so can result in substantial fines for organizations and particular attention should be paid to the requirement to keep data secure. The DPA creates something known as a section 55 criminal offence. Under section 55 of the DPA, '(1) A person must not knowingly or recklessly, without the consent of a Data Controller (a) obtain or disclose personal data or (b) procure the disclosure of personal data to another person'. All employee and consumer details will be covered by this requirement and, therefore, any security breach that, for instance, releases individual customer details onto the web would also be a breach of section 55(1) of the DPA and, therefore, a criminal offence. Of course, the DPA only applies if the Data Controller is established in the United Kingdom and/or the processing takes part in the United Kingdom; criminals based outside the EU and operating in breach of the DPA are able to do so with considerable impunity.

PRIVACY AND ELECTRONIC COMMUNICATIONS REGULATIONS 2003

These regulations came into force on 11 December 2003 and superseded the earlier Telecommunications (Data Protection and Privacy) Regulations 1999. The Information Commissioner is responsible for enforcing them and there is a section on his website dealing with these regulations.

The regulations cover use, by telecommunication network and service providers, and individuals, of any publicly available electronic communications network for direct marketing purposes, and any unsolicited direct marketing activity by telephone, fax, electronic mail (which includes text/video/picture messaging, SMS and e-mail) and by automated telephone calling systems. The key right conferred both on individuals and corporate entities is the right to register their objection to receiving unsolicited direct marketing material, and it provides a mechanism for doing this. A number of requirements, including in some circumstances the obligation to obtain the prior consent of the person to whom marketing messages are to be directed, are imposed on direct marketers and these will intersect with obligations under the DPA; organizations have to ensure that they comply with both. The Information Commissioner's website supplies, and keeps up to date, detailed guidance on these regulations. The detailed law around data protection and privacy is changing as cases work their way through the courts. Any organization engaged in direct electronic marketing of any sort needs to take appropriate legal advice and ensure that their operations remain in line with the law.

FREEDOM OF INFORMATION ACT 2000 (THE 'FOIA')

The Information Commissioner ALSO enforces the Freedom of Information Act. The FOIA provides a general right of access to all types of information held by UK public authorities and those providing services for them. The FOIA is 'intended to promote a culture of openness and accountability amongst public sector bodies, and therefore facilitate better public understanding of how public bodies carry out their duties, why they make the decisions they do, and how they spend public money'. Only public authorities are covered by the Act and there is a long list, at Schedule 1 of the FOIA, of all the organizations covered. It basically includes any public body.

The FOIA came fully into force on 1 January 2005 and the first adoption of a publication scheme under the FOIA was by government departments and their agencies in 2002. The rights of individuals to access information held by these organizations, and the responsibilities of the organizations, can be explored further on www.informationcommissioner.gov.uk.

Private companies should note that one of the clear consequences of the FOIA is that details of their previously confidential public sector tenders and contracts could now be made public, irrespective of any previous confidentiality clauses. This is a key area on which private sector companies may urgently need to take contract-specific professional advice; certainly, their commercial practices may need to be adjusted to reflect the risk of disclosure.

The Information Commissioner is also now responsible for the Environmental Information Regulations 2004 (which came into force on 1 January 2005), which enable people to access environmental information held by or on behalf of UK public authorities and those bodies carrying out a public function. Technically, any environmental information request is an FOIA request but, as environmental information was exempted in the FOIA, these regulations are necessary. As part of the requested information might also be personal information (for example, if the applicant is a subject of the information request), these regulations intersect with the DPA.

COMPUTER MISUSE ACT 1990 (THE 'CMA')

The Computer Misuse Act 1990 was designed to set up provisions for securing computer material against unauthorized access or modification. It created three offences: the first is to knowingly use a computer to obtain unauthorized access to any program or data held in the computer; the second is to use this unauthorized access to commit one or more offences; the third is to carry out an unauthorized modification of any computer material. The Act allows for penalties in the form of both fines and imprisonment.

The Act basically outlaws, within the United Kingdom, hacking and the introduction of computer viruses. It hasn't been entirely successful in doing so. It initially had a significant impact on the computer policies of universities, often seen as the source of much of this sort of activity. It does have other implications for computer users in the United Kingdom. Anyone using someone else's user name without proper authorization is potentially committing an offence. Anyone copying data, that is not specifically authorized to do so, is potentially committing an offence. It also has relevance for organizations whose employees may be using organizational facilities to hack other sites or otherwise commit offences identified under the Act. The organization should take full advantage of the RIPA (see below) to ensure that staff are complying with the law.

The UK's All Party Internet Group (APIG) reviewed this Act in mid-2004, recognized that it has been ineffective, largely through inadequate enforcement resourcing. It recommended a limited number of changes to the CMA as well as a number of other actions, by other bodies, to improve the legal environment for computer security.

COPYRIGHT, DESIGNS AND PATENTS ACT 1988 (THE 'CDPA')

The Internet starting point for organizations that want detailed advice on intellectual property is www.intellectual-property.gov.uk. The principal legislation on copyright can be found in the Copyright Designs and Patents Act 1988. It has been amended a number of times and there is no official consolidation of it. A list of the most important pieces of legislation that have amended the 1988 Act and some other information about the legislation can be obtained from the UK Patent Office (www.patent.gov.uk). This is a complex and difficult area for any organization that deals in intellectual property and appropriate professional advice should be taken from a firm that specializes in this area.

ELECTRONIC COMMUNICATIONS ACT 2000

This Act, along with the Electronic Signatures Regulations 2002 and the Electronic Commerce Regulations 2002, is designed to regulate the usage, within the United Kingdom, of cryptography and to make provision for the use of electronic signatures. Essentially, there are fallback powers (not yet exercised) to create a central, statutory but voluntary register of approved providers of cryptography services in the United Kingdom and there are a number of regulations affecting how these approvals are given. It also provides for appropriately authenticated electronic signatures to be used in electronic commerce and allows for them to be admitted as evidence in court.

HUMAN RIGHTS ACT 1998 (THE 'HRA')

The HRA was enacted in October 2000. It incorporates into UK law the principles of the European Convention for the Protection of Human Rights and Fundamental Freedoms (the Convention). Most of the rights within the Convention are qualified, insofar as they are subject to limitations if the employer can show necessity to protect the rights and freedom of others. In particular, an employee could argue in a court or tribunal that the employer monitoring or tapping the employee's work telephone or e-mail or internet activity was a breach of her/his rights under the Convention.

REGULATION OF INVESTIGATORY POWERS ACT 2000 (THE 'RIPA')

Section 1 of the RIPA makes it unlawful to intentionally intercept communications over a public or private telecommunications network without lawful authority. Section 3 allows a defence if it can be reasonably believed that both parties consented to the interception. The Telecommunications (Lawful Business Practice) (Interception of Communications) Regulations 2000 (the Regulations) were issued under the powers of the RIPA and these allow employers to monitor employee communications where the employee has not given express consent, provided that the monitoring is to:

- record evidence of business transactions;
- ensure compliance with regulatory or self-regulatory guidelines;
- maintain the effective operation of the employer's systems;
- monitor standards of training and service;
- prevent or detect criminal activity;
- prevent the unauthorized use of computer or telephone systems (ensuring that the employer's policies are not breached).

Employers also have to take reasonable steps to inform employees that their communications might be intercepted. This means that employers must introduce acceptable use policies that set out, for the employees, the right to monitor such communications.

Code of Practice

The Information Commissioner published a Code of Practice called 'The Use of Personal Data in Employer/Employee Relationships'. This code is more restrictive than the Regulations issued under the power of the RIPA. The Code argues that the interception of personal electronic communications will almost certainly be covered by Data Protection principles. It says that unless:

the circumstances justify the additional intrusion, [organizations should] limit monitoring to traffic data rather than the contents of the communication, undertake spot checks rather than continuous monitoring, as far as possible, automate the monitoring so as to reduce the extent to which extraneous information is made available to any person other than the parties to a communication, and target monitoring to areas of highest risk.

While there will certainly be a series of court and tribunal cases over the next few years that deal with the conflicts between the HRA, the RIPA and the Code, employers certainly need to introduce an acceptable use policy if they wish to be able to take legal or disciplinary action in respect of inappropriate employee behaviour.

INTELLECTUAL PROPERTY RIGHTS (IPR)

Organizations and individuals deal with all sorts of third-party material, some of which may contain IPR, in the form of copyright, design rights or trademarks. Copyright infringement can lead to legal action, even involving criminal proceedings, if there has been a clear breach of the CDPA. Organizations should, therefore, adopt appropriate controls to avoid this happening. There are, broadly speaking, two controls that might be adopted. The first is educational, ensuring that everyone in the organization understands the issues and takes action to avoid copyright infringement. Such an approach would require everyone to understand where the boundary between legal and illegal copying lies and what the requirements are, for instance, for identifying sources of information contained in new publications.

The second would be to simply ban anyone in the organization from using any material that wasn't developed within the organization. This, while keeping the slate very clean, might be unnecessarily limiting and the organization has to decide, in the light of a risk assessment, what its best course will be.

Software copyright

A most important issue in dealing with copyright is for the organization to ensure that it is not infringing the copyright of the suppliers of the software that it is using. Different software packages are licensed on different bases and the organization needs to be clear how each of its software packages is licensed and that it has paid for the correct number of **licences**.

There is also a wide range of 'freeware' available on the Internet, which is software that can be downloaded subject to specific licence terms. This includes plug-ins, such as Real Player, Macromedia Flash, etc. As these usually cannot be downloaded without the user accepting the licence conditions, there are not usually any licence-tracking issues here, although the organization ought to maintain a register of all such licences, to ensure that their terms are being complied with.

Organizations need to maintain a register of software licences, which lists all the licences that they own, as well as the purchase dates and, where appropriate, the disposal dates. The register should be updated wherever an upgrade is installed; a migration from (say) MS NT4 to MS Windows XP should be clearly noted in the register. The licences that are identified in the register should all be stored with the register and be available for an auditor to confirm their existence.

The organization should include, in the access agreement signed by each member of staff before they are allowed to access any organizational computer, a statement that only licensed and formally approved software may be used on the organization's computers and that any use of illegally obtained or unlicensed software will lead to disciplinary action. The organization will have to decide how to handle the wide range of freeware that is available across the Internet, as maintaining a ban on the installation of freely downloadable software may not be cost-effective. However, allowing anyone to download whatever they want may result in non-business-related programs appearing on the network and taking up valuable time, bandwidth and storage capacity. If these programs are then circulated internally by e-mail they could potentially cause a system crash as a result of system overload. This would be a security incident, as data required by the organization to pursue its objectives might become unavailable.

On a regular basis, the network administrator should carry out an audit of the software that is actually installed on the network PCs. This should be conducted at least annually, but experience shows that (particularly in fast changing or growing networks) this could usefully be done as often as every quarter. These audits can be carried out by centralized network administration software and, while this will deal with permanently connected PCs, it will be necessary to ensure that all notebooks are scanned on a regular basis as well. Records should be kept of these audits, demonstrating that all machines have been audited and showing what action, if any, has been taken to remove illegal software (or acquire additional licences where necessary) and to deal with offenders.

The Federation Against Software Theft (**FAST** – www.fast.org.uk) was set up in 1984 by the British Computer Society's Copyright Committee. It was the first software copyright organization. It has concentrated on raising the awareness of software piracy and lobbying Parliament for changes in the Copyright Act 1956 to reflect the needs of software authors and publishers. It represents both software publishers and end users and has a long history of working with both sides of the copyright relationship to ensure that software is properly managed. Corporations can join FAST, which provides a range of services designed to assist them to properly manage software and to comply with the law. FAST offers advice, assistance and training; it also offers an audit certificate that recognizes that the organization concerned is properly managing its software.

The comment that FAST made on its website (January 2002), about copyright and the law, should be noted:

> Software is covered by the laws of copyright and using software outside the terms of its licence can constitute either a civil and/or a criminal breach of copyright law. Many people are surprised to find that they can still be found guilty of copyright infringement even if they did not copy or distribute software for the purpose of direct commercial gain. Officers of a company are responsible for ensuring that their organization complies with the law. Ignorance is no defence. Even if a manager is totally unaware that software theft is occurring within his or her organization, that does not absolve the company from legal proceedings. In the recent past, those sued by software publishers have been forced to pay all the legal fees that have been incurred; pay damages to the copyright holder; remove all their illegal software and buy new, legal copies.

FAST is a member, together with a number of other trade and representative organizations in the United Kingdom, of the Alliance against Counterfeiting and Piracy (www.aacp.org.uk) with which it works on major legislative and campaigning issues. FAST has joined with other representative bodies in the film and music industries to create a single copyright advice and anti-piracy hotline (0845 603 4567, website www.copyright-info.org), which both provides advice and takes reports of suspected software infringements. FAST sets out, on its website, the basis on which it believes that anyone who decides to 'blow the whistle' on his/her employer for software infringement will be protected:

The Public Interest Disclosure Act (the 'Whistle Blowers Act') includes three basic requirements:

- The employee believes that their employer is committing a criminal offence or breach of civil law. Underlicensing falls within both these categories. The illegal use of software in a business, or a manager turning a blind eye to misuse, are both criminal offences. Software infringement such as buying one copy and using many is a civil infringement.
- The employee must believe that the disclosure is 'substantially' true, act in good faith and not make any personal gain. The Act has regard

to the identity of the person to whom the disclosure is made. A com-
plaint to FAST would be reasonable, whereas employees seeking a
fee from a newspaper may not be on such safe ground.

■ Was it reasonable in all the circumstances? For instance, could the
employee have brought the matter to the attention of the company
first without suffering detriment?

The implications of this should be clear for all organizations that are not
already committed to complying with the existing software legislation.
There is a very real risk that non-compliance will be exposed to FAST, to
AACP or a similar organization, perhaps by a disgruntled current or
former employee or competitor, with the potential consequences outlined
above.

There are similar private organizations, which are funded by the major
software manufacturers to combat illegal use of software. They target
organizations that they think may be using illegal software (which includes having more users of an off-the-shelf package than there are licences).
There is no legal requirement to comply with their demands and it is
appropriate to take legal advice before responding to any demands that
are made. It is always sensible, through the consistent application of an
effective software copyright policy, to ensure that the organization is
constantly able to demonstrate its compliance with the legislation and
with the terms of any software licences.

Finally, organizations need to have an appropriate policy in place to
deal with disposal of copyright material, which needs to be done in
accordance with the licences.

Safeguarding of organizational records

Some organizational and individual records must be retained to meet
statutory or regulatory requirements, while others may be needed to
provide adequate defence against potential civil or criminal action or to
prove the financial status of the organization to the range of potential
interested parties, including shareholders, tax authorities, auditors and
to meet contractual liabilities. Records do not (and should not) be kept
for ever – this can make it difficult to find what is required as and when it
is required.

Therefore, time limits should be set for the retention of individual
categories of information. After this time, records should be destroyed –
in line with the procedure adopted by the organization to ensure that any
confidential information within those records is not inadvertently made
public. Some time limits will be set by statute or regulation and the
organization should establish, with its legal advisers, what the current

categories of documents and retention requirements are. Both the Inland Revenue and HM Customs and Excise requirements should be met.

There is a substantial discussion, in Chapter 27 of *IT Governance: A Manager's Guide to Data Security and BS 7799/ISO 17799*, on record retention and readers are referred to that book for further guidance on this subject.

The ABC glossary of information security and related terms

Definitions that have been taken from ISO 17799:2005 are identified thus: *.

Definitions that have been taken from BS 7799:2002 are identified thus: **.

Key controls are indicated (**KC**); significant risks or threats are indicated (**SR**). Rule references here are to the Infosec Basics for Business. The Internet Highway Code uses the same definitions as the Infosec Basics.

Words in italics are cross-referenced to other entries in the glossary.

acceptable use policy (KC)   An acceptable use policy sets out what the organization considers acceptable behaviour on, and acceptable use of, e-mail and *internet* access systems. A number of legal, employment, *Human Rights Act* and *Regulation of Investigatory Powers Act* issues affect the development and deployment of acceptable use policies, but this should not deter organizations from putting them in place. See Chapter 4, rule 7.

access   The opportunity (either physical or *logical* or both) to use any *information processing facilities* or any component of them (for example, a piece of data, an *application*, etc).

access agreement (KC)   This is an agreement, between an organization and each of its employees, issued prior to release of a specific *user name*, in which the employee accepts the *access rights* and *privileges* attached to that user name and agrees to follow a series of procedures and requirements in respect of the use of that user name. This usually includes agreement to comply with the *acceptable use policy*. See Chapter 4, rule 7.

access control (KC)   This is the policy of controlling *access* to *information processing facilities* through a combination of *access agreements* and technological security measures that implement the policy *guidelines*. These *controls* therefore restrict the rights of individual *users* to access information processing facilities. User *access rights* reflect user access controls: the user has the right to do those things that the controls allow. See Chapter 4, rule 7.

access control list (ACL)   A formal (preferably approved) list of *users* that have defined *access rights* to an *asset* within *information processing facilities*; in other words, it ensures that only legitimate users can access the asset.

access point (AP)   This is the piece of radio hardware that enables *wireless* computers to access a wired (or fixed) *network*.

access rights   Are usually determined by a *policy* that *users* should only have *access* to those *systems* and *assets* that they need in order to do their jobs and that everything else is expressly forbidden to them. These access rights are usually enforced through the *user agreement* and in how the systems are configured.

accountability (KC)   Not obviously a computer-related term, but fundamental to effective *information security* and is the concept that any activity within an *information system* should be traceable to an individual that can be held responsible for the action (or inaction) and its consequences. It is the notion that the 'buck stops somewhere'. See Chapter 4, rule 2.

ACL   See *access control list*.

ActiveX   A Microsoft ActiveX control is a 'component object model technology' that is designed to enable software components to communicate. It allows *users* to quickly and easily download added functionality to *Internet Explorer* and is often exploited by *spyware*.

ad hoc mode   A method of connecting up to nine *wireless clients* directly to one another, without the use of a *wireless AP*.

administrator   This is the *user* role that is responsible for installation, *configuration*, update, amendment or deletion of a *system*, usually a software system. An administrator can do anything, usually untraceably, and therefore administrator *user names* should only be issued to people of proven competence who have been successfully screened to ensure there is no history of malicious computer-related activity.

Advanced Encryption Standard (AES)   Also known as 'Rijndael', a portmanteau word formed from the names of its two inventors, this US government 128-*bit encryption* standard superseded *DES* in November 2001 and is widely deployed.

advisory   Organizations such as *CERT* issue these. An advisory is an assessment of significant new *information security* trends or developments and may relate to broad trends or specific *threats* and technologies.

adware (SR)   Advertising that is integrated into software and which is usually provided as a download to a computer in combination with another *application* provided at no charge provided the adware is run. Adware is sometimes malicious.

AES   See *Advanced Encryption Standard*.

airborne viruses (SR)   These are *viruses* that use short range *wireless* connections (for example, *Bluetooth*) for propagation. Mobile phones and *PDA*s are the targets of this sort of virus.

analogue   'Relating to or using information represented by a continuously variable physical quality (such as spatial position, voltage, etc) rather than digitally' is the definition provided in the *OED* (Concise, 11th Edition); if the computer world of *bits* and *bytes* is the *digital* one, the physical world in which we live, eat and breathe is the analogue one.

anti-malware software (KC)   This is software specifically developed to deal with *malware*: *adware, spam, spim, spyware, Trojans, viruses, worms* and most automated *exploits*, irrespective of their attack *vector*. This term should not be seen as synonymous with *anti-virus software*, not all of which adequately reflects the range of ways in which individuals and organizations connect to the *internet*. A good anti-virus software package will deal with all aspects of malware except for adware and spyware, which will need their own solutions. See Chapter 4, rule 6.

anti-spyware   Software that will identify *spyware* packages that are installed on a computer and, if given the instruction by the *user*, will then remove all instance of them from the computer – wherever they are hiding.

anti-virus software (KC):

1. Anti-virus software is software that is specifically designed to detect and halt *viruses, worms* and *Trojans* in e-mail. It is not necessarily designed to deal with *spyware, adware, spam,* or anything coming through *instant messaging* software.

2. Anti-virus software tackles viruses at three points: it examines incoming e-mail (particularly attachments) at your e-mail *gateway* for known *viruses*; it scans the hard disk and all the files for any viruses that may have bypassed the *g*ateway virus checker; and it scans outgoing e-mails to ensure they are not carrying an infection.

3. There are two types of virus detection. The first relies on identifying precise characteristics of viruses (by searching for their 'signatures' and comparing them with its database of known viruses) and the second (*heuristic* detection) searches for types of misbehaving programs. New worms are more likely to be detected by heuristic checks.

4. Normal viruses are only going to be detected if your anti-virus software has an up-to-date database of signatures. This means regular *updates*; daily is better than once per week.

5. Tip: allow the *automatic update* service to run the moment it alerts you; a large proportion of viruses and other *exploits* propagate themselves via computers that don't yet have the latest updates installed.

6. Installing more than one anti-virus software package WILL NOT increase your protection – it may even decrease your protection if the packages conflict.

7. Windows XP Service Pack 2 does not contain anti-virus software. It will alert you if your anti-virus software is not running, or is not up to date, but that is all.
8. Today's *blended threats* mean that your anti-virus software must integrate with your *firewall* and other *anti-malware* software (anti-spam, *anti-spyware*, instant message protection, etc): unless you are a sophisticated *user*, you are better off finding and installing a package that covers all the bases rather than attempting to configure a number of different packages from a number of different suppliers to work together; if your current supplier hasn't worked out how to do it, you might look for one who can.

AP See *access point*.

applet A small *Java* program that runs in a *browser*. Applets are designed so that they cannot read or write to the browser's computer file system or open any other *network* connections.

application (or **application software**) This is the software that *users* actually use – Microsoft Office, or SAP, for instance.

application layer The standard *TCP/IP model*'s top layer, providing *protocols* for services such as e-mail, file transfer, etc.

Application Service Provider (ASP) An organization that provides *application* software on an outsourced, or rental basis.

architecture The broad outline of a *network* (or a computer, or a software program) into which the detailed processes will be placed. An open architecture is one that allows for easy connection by devices from other manufacturers, while a proprietary architecture is designed to make this difficult.

archive See *auto-archive*.

Arpanet The Advanced Research Project Agency ran the first computer *network* in the 1970s. The *internet* evolved from Arpanet, which was switched off in 1990.

ASCII American Standard Code for Information Interchange.

ASP See *Application Service Provider*.

asset Anything that has value to the organization.* Information assets are likely to be of the following types:

1. *information*: databases and data files, other files and copies of plans, *system* documentation, original *user* manuals, original training material, operational or other support procedures, continuity plans and other fallback arrangements, archived information, financial and accounting information;
2. software: *application* software, *operating* and system software, development tools and utilities, e-learning assets, network tools and utilities;
3. physical *assets*: computer equipment (including workstations, notebooks, *PDAs*, monitors, *modems*, scanning machines, *printers*), com-

munications equipment (*routers*, *cellphones*, PABXs, fax machines, answering machines, voice conferencing units, etc), magnetic media (tapes and disks), other technical equipment (power supplies, air conditioning units), furniture, lighting, other equipment;

4. services: 'groups of assets which act together to provide a particular function', such as computing and communications services, general utilities, for example, heating, lighting, power, air conditioning.

asymmetric encryption   Also known as *public key encryption*, a system under which an organization has two *keys*, one private and one public. Anyone can use the *public key* to encrypt a message for the organization, knowing that only the possessor of the *private key* will be able to *decrypt* it. Equally, anything that decrypts properly using the public key must have been encrypted using the complementary private key. A critical issue in public key *cryptography* is to attest the validity of the key pair and, in particular, that the named public key really is the organization's public key. This is done with a *digital certificate*, issued by a *certificate authority*.

authentication (KC)   This is the process of establishing that *users* are who they claim to be. It requires users to provide a combination of a *user name* and one or more credentials: something known (a *password*), something possessed (*digital signatures*, *smart cards*), or a physical feature (*biometrics*). Weak authentication requires just a password; strong authentication (*two factor authentication*) requires at least two of these three types of credential. 'Authenticity' is a description of an authenticated user. See Chapter 4, rule 7.

authorization (KC)   Once a user has been authenticated, authorization to use the *information*, computer services or other *system* can be granted. A system's authorized user file identifies who has what access rights. Authorization also applies to the step prior to granting of a *user name*, when an organization authorizes an individual to have specific *access rights*. See Chapter 4, rule 7.

auto-archive   An automated process of archiving old digital material, particularly e-mail.

auto-dialler (SR)   Small software program that automatically dials a designated telephone number in order to connect a *user* to their *ISP*. This might be set up by design through Windows, or it might be an option offered while visiting a website. The latter are usually premium rate numbers and the cost of the calls is automatically added to the user's *ISP* or telephone bill. There are *Trojans* that change your autodial settings to the more expensive ones.

automated hacking script (KC)   A method of exploiting a *vulnerability* in software that has been turned into a piece of autonomous code and released onto the *internet*.

automatic updates (KC)   A software provider's automated process for issuing updates (*patches*, fixes and *upgrades*) to their installed base of *users*, such that the update is executed with a minimum of user involvement. See Chapter 4, rule 9.

availability   Ensuring that authorized *users* have access to *information* and associated *assets* when required**.

awareness training (KC)   All employees of any organization that uses computers need to be trained in their safe use and be kept aware of *threats* and responses to them. The *Internet Highway Code* provides basic training and employers should send out regular awareness updates to their staff. See Chapter 4, rule 14.

back door (SR)   Programmers or *administrators* deliberately leave ways into software *systems* that can be used later to allow *access* to the system while bypassing the authorized user file. Sometimes, developers forget to take out something that was put there simply to ease development work or to assist with the debugging routine. Sometimes they are deliberately left in to help field engineers maintain the system. However they get there, they can provide any unauthorized user with access to the system.

back orifice   A remote administration tool that has great potential for malicious use. It is very easy to use, so that *script kiddies* have no problem using it. It is also 'extensible', which means that it develops and improves with age. Most *anti-malware* systems should detect and remove back orifice, but new versions become available on a regular basis.

backup (KC) (*PDAs*, computers, networks)   A backup is a copy of *information* that is made and retained in case of loss or damage to the original – it could be paper copies of paper documents, but we are mostly concerned with *digital* copies of digital data – which includes all information *assets*: *client* and supplier data, business planning data, *intellectual property*, *operating systems*, *applications*, *protocols*, everything. See Chapter 4, rule 11.

backup cycles   A copy just of tonight's data is useful, but neither efficient nor adequate. Not efficient, because a complete *backup* will take substantial time to run and will require a lot of tape. Not useful, because you may need (for *forensic* reasons, for instance) to *access* an older version of the data – and you don't want to have hundreds and hundreds of backup tapes. A backup cycle usually works on a grandfather, father, son basis. The 'son' is an incremental daily backup, collecting details only of today's changes, and the tape is reused on the same day next week; the 'father' backup is done at the end of every week (one tape for each day) and is overwritten at the end of the same week next month. The 'grandfather' backups are done at the end of every month and are overwritten in the same month next year. Remember, backup has nothing to do with *data retention policies*; data retention policies are driven by local compliance requirements. Whatever data has to be retained, also has to be backed up.

bandwidth   The amount of data that a particular data cable can carry at any one time.

Basel 2   The Committee for Bank Supervision's most recent revision to the Basel risk-based capital rules for banks.

BCM   See *business continuity management*.

biometrics   The identification of a *user* by means of a physical characteristic, such as a fingerprint, iris, face or voice.

bit   This is a unit of measurement of *information* (from **b**inary + dig**it**); there are eight bits in a *byte*.

bit-wiping software   Software that will, under certain conditions, wipe out specific data stored on a device.

Blackberry   A hand-held wireless e-mail device.

black hat   A type of *hacker*.

blacklist   List with negative connotations: for instance, it might be a list of those senders that a *spam filter* will ALWAYS filter out, or a list of those *cellphones* that will be banned from connecting to the cellphone network.

blended threat (SR)   This might more accurately be described as the *threat* of a blended attack, an attack that comes from a number of directions, or via a number of *vectors*. For instance, a *spam* e-mail message might be carrying a *payload*, in the form of a *Trojan*, which it installs on your computer to open it up to a *botnet*. Similarly, an innocent-looking piece of *adware* might contain some *spyware*, a Trojan installer and a *browser* hijacker.

bluejacking (SR)   An attack on a *Bluetooth*-enabled device (usually a mobile phone) in which an attacker sends an unauthorized message to the device.

blue screen   When *Microsoft*'s Windows *operating system* snarled up on some internal software fault and became incapable of continuing, the *user* would usually get a blue screen (aka the 'blue screen of death'). Any work you were doing was lost and you had to switch off and re-*boot*. Now it just freezes.

bluesnarfing (SR)   An attack on a *Bluetooth*-enabled device that allows download of all contact details along with other information without leaving any trace of the attack.

Bluetooth   A radio-frequency standard that allows any sort of electronic equipment to make its own short-range connections, without wires, cables or direct action of any sort from a *user*. It is an inexpensive, *wireless* and hassle-free technology that is being deployed in a vast range of *digital* equipment. The name 'Bluetooth' refers to the 8th-century Danish king, Harald Bluetooth, who united Denmark and Norway and introduced Christianity into Denmark. He had little to do with communication technology, but Scandinavian companies have long been a driving force behind the development of mobile telephony and the development of this standard. Bluetooth is not restricted to line-of-sight, but its effective range is about 10 metres; this short range is a result of its very weak signal, selected to avoid the danger of interference with other devices – primarily medical ones – that use the same range of frequencies. However, longer range Bluetooth snooping devices are emerging.

Bluetooth snarfing   See *bluesnarfing*.

boot   The process that takes place inside the computer after you switch it on and it starts loading your operating system while you do something else – it comes from the idea of a bootstrap as something that you use to pull your boots on with.

bots   Short for ro**bots**.

botnets   This is a *network* of *zombie* computers, usually created and controlled by criminals, either for distributing *spam* or for mounting *DDoS* attacks.

broadband   High *bandwidth* cable.

browser (*IE*, *Firefox*, Opera)   This is the piece of software that enables a *user* to browse sites on the web. *Microsoft's Internet Explorer* is the most widely used; Firefox and Opera are two *open-source* competitors.

brute force attack   See *password cracking*.

BS 7799   A specification for an *Information Security Management System* based on the best practice guidance of *ISO 17799*, conformance with which provides grounds for external, *third-party certification* of the quality of an organization's *information security* posture.

BS 7799:2005 (KC)   The revised version of *BS 7799-2* issued in 2005 with an Annex A updated to reflect the revisions to *ISO 17799:2005*. Organizations seeking *certification* to BS 7799 must be compliant with BS 7799-2:2005 and already certified organizations have to *upgrade* their *ISMSs* to the BS 7799-2:2005 standard before their three-yearly reassessments. ISO 27001:2005 is the international version of BS7799-2:2005.

BSA   The **B**usiness **S**oftware **A**lliance is 'the foremost organization dedicated to promoting a safe and legal *digital* world', which it does by pursuing organizations that might be running unlicensed software.

b2b   Business-to-business.

b2c   Business-to-consumer.

buffer overflow (SR) (or overrun)   A buffer is an area of memory that holds data to be processed. It has a fixed, predetermined size. If too much data are placed into the buffer, they can be lost or can overwrite other, legitimate data. Buffer overflow vulnerabilities have for a number of years been a major method of *intrusion*. They provide *hackers* with an opportunity to load and execute malicious code on a target *workstation*.

Bugtraq   A regularly updated 'high volume, full disclosure mailing list for the detailed discussion and announcement of computer security vulnerabilities'. It is a vendor-neutral, central store of known *operating system* vulnerabilities; the website is at www.securityfocus.com/archive/1. Anyone can read the latest vulnerability disclosures – including cyber-criminals.

business continuity management   The creation, management and maintenance of an organization's *business continuity plan*.

business continuity plan (KC)   This is a scenario-based plan, developed in advance of any incidents that might undermine the availability of an organization's *information*, and which describes precisely how each of the most likely incidents is to be handled. It usually involves specific infrastructure and system amendments that will make continuity possible, and it certainly requires regular testing, to ensure that it will actually work when the time comes. Also see *disaster recovery plan*ning and Chapter 4, rule 11.

byte   Eight *bits*.

cache   This is the section of a computer's memory that retains recently accessed data in order to speed up repeated *access* to the same data. If the data on the web has altered since you last visited it, you may need to refresh the page to see the new data, otherwise you will only see what is stored in the cache.

Can-Spam   The US act against spam. See Chapter 9.

cellphones   See *mobile phones*.

CERT   Computer Emergency Response Team – the *internet* emergency response team formed by the US Defense Advanced Research Projects Agency (DARPA).

certificate authority (CA)   A trusted *third party* that will issue a *digital certificate* to attest the authenticity of an organization's *public key*. The CA will review the credentials of any organization that wants a digital certificate before issuing it. This review will include the Dun and Bradstreet number or Articles of Incorporation and a thorough background check to ensure that the organization is what it claims to be. The CA may be a secure *server* on the *network* (the single trust model) or an external *third-party* organization recognized by many (the multi-party trust model). The *keys* used are either 40-*bit* or 128-bit.

certification   A *third-party* audit organization can examine the extent to which an organization's *ISMS* meets the specification of *BS 7799* and, if it does, it can issue a certificate of compliance.

challenge-response   A technique for fighting *spam*, which requires a new sender to prove legitimacy to the recipient by entering a code on a website.

change control   The process and procedures to identify, document, review and authorize any changes to software, documents, projects, etc.

CHAP   Challenge Handshake Authentication Protocol – a method of *authentication* between a *server* and a *client*.

chat room   A virtual room, on the web, in which *users* can chat.

CIS   The Center for Internet Security – a standard setter for secure *configuration* of systems connected to the *internet*, and its website is at www.cisecurity.org.

CISSP Certificate for Information System Security Professional, a certificate for *information security* practitioners.

classification system (KC) A system where *information assets* are classified and clearly marked according to their sensitivity, *confidentiality*, value, importance, etc. This subject is very thoroughly covered in *IT Governance: A Manager's Guide to Data Security and BS 7799/ISO 17799* and a basic system is outlined in Chapter 4 (Infosec Basic 3).

client A computer that uses a *server* or a *network* service for something that it cannot do on its own.

cloaking bags Bags that are designed to block *WiFi* and *Bluetooth* signals and which can protect 'always on' *cellphones* and *PDAs* from signal leakage or hijacking.

'commercial in confidence' This is a classification level for information. It is not clear what purpose it serves, other than to highlight to someone that receives it that it may have value on the black market. An *information security classification system* needs to be simple, practical and coherent. See *classification system* as well as Chapter 4, rule 3, for an outline of such a system.

Common Criteria (CC) The 'CC defines a set of IT requirements of known validity, which can be used in establishing security requirements for prospective products and *systems*' and the official CC website is at www.commoncriteriaportal.org.

compartmentalization The concept of an internally secure *network* designed with a number of cooperating sub-networks and light *firewalls* and *routers*.

compliance A positive answer to the question: 'Is what is taking place in line with the pre-specified requirements for what should take place?' Hence, non-compliance and compliance monitoring.

Computer Misuse Act See Chapter 9.

computer security See *information security* – because ensuring that the physical hardware, the computer, is secure, is part of the overall job of ensuring that all the *information* is secure. Computer security is just a part of the whole job. See also the discussion of information insecurity in the first three sections of Chapter 4.

confidentiality Ensuring that *information* is accessible only to those authorized to have *access***.

configuration How the components of a computer or a *network* are set up.

contracts See 'security in contracts' in Chapter 4, rule 4.

control Means of managing risk, including *policies, procedures, guidelines*, practices or organizational structures, which can be of administrative, technical, management or legal nature; also used as a synonym for safeguard or countermeasure*.

controlled document   One that is version controlled in line with a document control system such as the one contained in ISO 9000:2000.

control objective   The *risk treatment plan* objective that is to be achieved by implementing one or more of a number of *control*s.

control standard   The level to which it has been decided that a *risk* must be controlled; this is usually determined by balancing the cost of the *control*, the likelihood of the risk and its potential *impact* to determine how much should be invested in controlling it. This cost of control (which should not exceed the likely cost of the *impact*) is translated into a standard against which the effectiveness of the control can be assessed.

cookie   This is a small data file that a website stores on a surfer's computer and which contains *information* about the *user* (for example, user preferences) that is relevant to the user's experience of the website.

copyright   See Chapter 9.

Copyright Designs and Patents Act 1988   See Chapter 9.

covert channels (SR) – those channels installed, usually by software developers, in order to simplify the process of getting back into a piece of code, in order to amend it. These channels can be exploited by *hackers*.

CPU   Central Processor Unit – this drives your computer.

crackers (SR)   *Hackers* who break into computer *system*s specifically to steal data or cause damage. Hackers like to say that crackers break in, but that hackers get permission first and will publish their discoveries. Hence: crack and cracking.

crash   This is what software sometimes does – see *blue screen*.

credit cards   Pieces of plastic that enable people to get into debt; they are also essential for online shopping.

credit reports   Summary of financial *information* about consumers assembled on the basis of information filed with credit reporting companies, primarily by lenders.

crime   See *cybercrime*.

critical   'Having a decisive importance in the success or failure of something' (*OED*, Concise, 11th Edition, 2004).

critical infrastructure   This is the construct of foundation *system*s and services that citizens and businesses rely on for their health, safety and well-being. Telecommunications, transportation, energy and banking services are part of the critical infrastructure, which is often privately owned but which governments believe that citizens expect them to protect.

cryptography   The art of protecting *information* by encrypting it.

CVE   Common Vulnerabilities and Exposures – the website at www.cve.mitre.org (funded by the US Department of Homeland Security) holds a dictionary 'of standardized names for vulnerabilities and other *information security* exposures, with the aim of standardizing the names for all publicly known vulnerabilities and security exposures'. It is not a database and would normally be used in conjunction with a *vulnerability* database like

Bugtraq. CVE is publicly available and free to use. Therefore, you should assume that cyber-criminals use it.

cybercrime (SR)   Any form of illegal activity that takes place in cyber-space. The UK's *Computer Misuse Act 1990* made it an offence for anyone to access a computer without *authorization*, to modify the contents of a computer without authorization, or to facilitate (allow) such activity to take place. It identified sanctions for such activity, including fines and imprisonment. Other countries have taken similar action to identify and create offences that should enable law enforcement bodies to deal with computer misuse.

cyberspace   Another term for the *digital* world, as opposed to the *analogue* one.

cyber-terrorism   Terrorist activities in *cyberspace*.

cyber trust   *Cyberspace* is still an inherently untrustworthy realm, in which it is not possible for buyers and sellers to physically establish one another's bona fides. Methods of establishing cyber trust are therefore essential for effective *e-commerce*.

cyber war   War in *cyberspace*, conducted by the military equivalents of *hackers*, spammers and *virus writers*.

Data Controller   The person, within an organization, who is responsible for the organization's compliance with the *Data Protection Act* – see Chapter 9.

Data Encryption Standard (DES)   A widely used *symmetric encryption* standard. It is used for long communications and is relatively speedy to use. It is, however, quite an old system and this has led to triple DES (or *AES*), in which the same data are encrypted three times, employing differ-ent *keys*, which exponentially increases the strength of the *encryption*. Only the creator and receiver have the DES key (or keys); the key(s) are usually exchanged using either a shared master key or a pre-existing key exchange protocol.

Data Protection Act (DPA)   See Chapter 9.

data retention policies   In each jurisdiction (and sometimes for each individual regulation or statute) there are very specific requirements about the period of time for which organizations have to retain particular types of data. These requirements form the basis of the organizational data retention policy, which will then require technological and procedural elements for its implementation. It will also give rise to data storage and *backup* issues. Also see Chapter 9.

DDoS   See *distributed denial of service attack*.

decryption   This is the opposite of *encryption*, and involves translating encrypted content back into its original (usually plain text) form.

defence in depth   See *layered security*.

denial of service attack (SR) (DOS) This sort of attack is designed to put an organization out of business – or to interrupt the activities of an individual or group of individuals – for a time by freezing its *systems*. This is usually done by flooding a web *server* (or other device) with e-mail messages or other data so that it is unable to provide a normal service to authorized *users*.

DES See *Data Encryption Standard*.

dialler Software (usually on a website) that will dial out to another website and charge back to you (on a *credit card* or, more usually, on your existing telephone bill) for the time used while on that site. The charge rate will not necessarily be lower than that of your existing supplier. See *auto-dialler*.

dictionary attack See *password cracking*.

digital An adjective describing an electronic device, process or datum that operates on, or is made up of, *information* in the form of numbers.

digital certificate (Sometimes called a server ID) is an encrypted file that attests to the authenticity of the owner of a *public key*, used in *public key encryption*; the certificate is created by a trusted *third party* known as a *certificate authority* (CA). The digital certificate is proven to be authentic because it decrypts correctly using the public key of the CA.

Digital Millennium Copyright Act (DMCA) See Chapter 9.

Digital Rights Management (DRM) Any technology that copyright owners might deploy to protect their interests in software or *digital* content. The technology only allows someone who has purchased a licence to use the material that it is protecting.

digital signature Encrypted data that binds a sender's identity to the *digital information* that is being transmitted. It is essential for *non-repudiation*.

digital watermarking Another term for *steganography* and is likely to become an important part of copyright management on the *internet*. There are a number of companies offering competing digital watermarking technologies, both to create and to view digital watermarks.

directory harvesting (SR) *Outlook* and other e-mail *client* software contain directories of individual names and e-mail addresses. Directory harvesting attacks commandeer these directories and use them for the distribution of *spam*, *viruses* or *worms*.

Disability Discrimination Act (DDA) This UK statute has clauses that require websites to be accessible to people with disabilities.

disaster recovery plan (KC) This is a scenario-based plan developed to deal with the after-effects of an 'act of nature'. Business continuity and disaster recovery planning should go hand-in-hand, otherwise one could spend far too long arguing over whether restoration of systems from the *backup* is part of the disaster recovery or the *business continuity plan*.

Certainly, disaster recovery management (or DRM) is about planning for and testing – usually rehearsing specific scenarios – potential disasters, such as fire, flood, terrorist explosion, etc.

disclaimers Not necessarily worth the (*digital*) paper on which they are written, but they are nevertheless an essential statement of ownership and intended destination of information sent electronically.

distributed denial of service attack (SR) (DDoS) This uses the computers of other, *third-party* organizations or individuals (which have themselves been commandeered by the *hacker*) to mount an even larger-scale *denial of service attack* on a target.

DMCA See *Digital Millennium Copyright Act.*

DMZ Demilitarized zone (the term has a military origin, meaning the buffer zone between two enemies) – this is a computer or small *network* between the organization's secure *perimeter* (the trusted zone is inside this perimeter) and an *untrusted* zone, such as the *internet*. Typically, the DMZ contains devices accessible to internet traffic, such as web *servers*, FTP servers, e-mail servers and DNS servers.

document control A *system* whereby all documents within the system have a standard numbering system that identifies where they sit within that system, as well as version number, an issue date and a document owner, so that the currency of the document is always clear. When a *controlled document* is amended, all copies of it should be simultaneously withdrawn and replaced by the new version.

domain controller A domain contains a number of resources (*applications*, folders, p*rinters*, etc) and a domain controller is the *server* that manages the details of all the *users* authorized to *access* the domain.

domain name Every website and e-mail address has a unique *IP address*, which, when represented in letters (for example, www.itgovernance. co.uk), is its domain name.

Domain Name Server (DNS) This is a *server* that translates *domain names* into *IP addresses*.

download Transfer a copy of a file (which may be data or a software program) from a remote computer (usually a website) to a requesting computer via a *network* (or *internet*) connection.

DPA See *Data Protection Act.*

e-commerce Trading in *cyberspace*, with goods and services usually supplied through a website.

e-crime See *cybercrime.*

e-crime busting This is the job of a country's High Tech Crime Unit. Any large organization should ensure that it has the contact details for its national body, so that it can report crimes quickly.

802.11 The *IEEE's* tag for a family of standards for *wireless LANs*, broken down into a number of different versions, adopted at different times.

802.11a   The *wireless* standard operating at 5 *GHz* and running at up to 54 *Mbps*. This was the second wireless standard adopted. It is not compatible with the other wireless standards, has a comparatively short range, at 30 metres, and is mostly used in office environments.

802.11b   The *wireless* standard that was originally known as *WiFi*. It operates at 2.4 *GHz* and at up to 11 *Mbps*. It has been widely adopted and is the most widely available and used, is compatible with *802.11g* and has a maximum outdoor range of about 120 metres and 50 metres indoors.

802.11g   The *wireless* standard operating at 2.4*GHz* but running at 54 *Mbps*; it is compatible with *802.11b* but is five times faster. An 802.11g device can *access* an *802.11b HotSpot*, but will run at the slower speed.

802.11i   The *wireless* standard that uses the more secure *AES*, a more secure method of handling *authentication*. This version was specifically developed to tackle the security issues that had emerged with earlier versions and is only recently becoming commercially available.

802.1X   Should not be confused with any *802.11* standards. 802.1X provides a framework for authenticating and authorizing devices connected to a *network* and would usually involve an *authentication server*. It improves security by automatically and dynamically changing *encryption keys* more quickly that any *hacker* can crack them.

Electronic Communications Act 2000   See Chapter 9.

electronic contracts   An electronically established legal contract – see Chapter 9.

e-mail authentication   As it is now possible to spoof an e-mail sender's name and address details, the question of how to authenticate the sender is becoming very important.

encryption (KC)   The conversion of plain text into code, using a mathematical algorithm, to prevent it from being read by a *third party*.

endpoint device   An endpoint device is a *PDA*, a *cellphone* or a laptop – a device that connects (usually but not necessarily) wirelessly to the *network*. Every endpoint device is a potential *vulnerability* for a network and, therefore, the network *perimeter* has to be considered as ending at the point of the device, rather than simply at the network *firewall*.

endpoint security (KC)   Security that is effective on all *endpoint devices*. See Chapter 7.

espionage (SR)   Most of the traditional cold war spy organizations are now actively involved in commercial spying, competing with their long-established private sector brethren.

Eudora   A popular e-mail program that works on both PCs and Macs, and is available as both *freeware* and an enterprise version.

event   An identified occurrence in a *system*, service or *network* indicating a possible breach of *information security policy* or failure of safeguards, or a previously unknown situation that may be security relevant* (see also *incident*).

evil twin (SR)   An attack in which an unauthorized or rogue *AP* with a stronger signal is placed in close proximity to a legitimate *AP*. *Wireless users* unwittingly log into the rogue AP (which might have a deliberately comforting *SSID*, such as 'local friendly coffee shop') and give away *passwords*, bank details and other sensitive information.

exploit   This is either the methodology for making an attack against an identified *vulnerability* (the noun) or the act (the verb) of attacking or exploiting the vulnerability. Exploits are often published on the *internet*, either by *black hats* or by *grey hats* who claim that this is a good way of forcing software suppliers to develop more secure software or to provide fixes for existing software. Exploits can be automated and released into the *wild*, just like a *virus*.

extranet   This is an extension to an organization's internal network, usually placed outside the organization's core *firewall* and secure *perimeter* but itself protected from unauthorized *access*, so that the organization's trusted partners have limited access to specific information and services.

FAST   The Federation Against Software Theft – see Chapter 9.

file sharing   The public sharing of files across a *network*, so that a number of *users* are able to *access* and use the same file.

filter   A software pattern or mask that is designed so that some types of items can pass through it while others will be caught and prevented or discarded.

Firefox   An *open-source browser*.

firewall (KC)   A technology that is designed to create a definite barrier and separation between two parts of a *network*, or between a network (or individual computer) and the *internet*. It filters traffic through its *ports* in line with its traffic filtering rules, which are set by the computer *user* or network *administrator* in line with corporate *guidelines*. See Chapter 4, rule 8.

flash   An animation technology from Macromedia; it can be watched through a *browser*.

flash cards (or flash sticks)   Devices that use *flash memory*.

flash memory   A non-volatile memory device that retains its data when the power is removed.

forensics   The scientific examination of evidence and applying that evidence to identify the commission, nature and perpetrator of a crime.

Freedom of Information Act (FoIA)   See Chapter 9.

freeware   This is software that is available on the *internet*, and can be downloaded for free. This free download may be conditional on you downloading an *adware* program, which may come bundled with a number of *scumware applications*.

gateway   Technically, hardware or software that translates between two dissimilar *protocols* and, often, any mechanism that provides *access* from one *system* to another (for example, between a *network* and the *internet*).

GHz   The Gigahertz (1,000,000,000 hertz) is a unit of frequency of ultra-high-frequency electromagnetic signals and is also a measure of micro-processor clock speeds.

GIAC   Global Information Assurance Certification – this is a certificate from the SANS Institute that provides assurance that a certified individual holds the appropriate level of knowledge and skill necessary to a practitioner in *information security*. The website is at www.giac.org.

GLBA   See Gramm-Leach-Bliley in Chapter 9.

Google   The largest *internet* search engine company. To 'google' is to use a *browser*-based search engine to find data on the *web*.

GPRS   General Packet Radio Service – this is part of the GSM standard and it delivers 'always-on' *wireless packet* data services to *GSM* customers; *users* only pay for the amount of data sent or received.

grey hat   A type of *hacker*.

GSM   Global System for Mobile Communication – a mobile pan-European *digital* cellular radio-communications *system*.

guest   A type of *user name* that is set up to allow those who have not been allocated their own specific user names to *access* and use a computer. It can easily be exploited by *hackers* and should be disabled.

guideline   A description that clarifies what should be done and how, to achieve the objectives set out in *policies**.

hackers (SR)   Hackers break into computer systems. Unlike *crackers*, they claim that they get permission first and will publish the results of their 'research'. Hackers have four prime motivations: challenge, to solve a security puzzle and outwit an identified security set-up; mischief, wanting to inflict stress or damage on an individual or organization; working around, getting around bugs or other blocks in a software system; and theft, stealing money or information. Hackers like to talk about *'white hat'* and *'black hat'* hackers; the argument is that the 'black hat' hackers are malicious and destructive (that is, *'crackers'*) while the 'white hat' hackers simply enjoy the challenge and are really on the side of good, offering their skills to help organizations test and defend their networks. This differentiation is convenient for hackers, who seem able to change hats as easily as they evade most network defences. The only sensible approach for any security-conscious organization is to assume that all hackers are potentially in the wrong colour hat, however they might initially present themselves. *'Grey hats'* is a term that is evolving to recognize the uncertain danger of so-called 'ethical' hackers. Nowadays, common sense suggests that a hacker is not to be trusted. See also *penetration testing*.

hacking tools   See www.insecure.org/tools.html for the current 75 most favourite tools for breaching (or assessing) the security of an organization, a website or a communication.

hand scanner   A hand-sized device that can be used for scanning documents for later upload to a computer.

hard drive   The permanent data storage device built into a workstation that stores its *operating system*, *applications*, other software and provides storage for files and folders. Its size is usually expressed in gigabytes.

heuristic   A method of detecting *viruses* that have not yet been formally identified (discovered and signatures defined) on the basis of their behaviour patterns.

HIPAA   Health Insurance Portability and Accountability Act – see Chapter 9.

history (in *browser*)   Your browser keeps a record of the websites you've visited, as an aide to your easy return. It can also be an aide for someone who wants to know where you've been – particularly in an *internet café*.

hoax   An e-mail message warning of a non-existent *virus* (or other problem) passed on by people who themselves received it and were duped into believing it was genuine. See *virus hoax*.

homeland security   The US now has a Department of Homeland Security, which is responsible for securing both the *analogue* and the *digital* borders of the United States.

honey pot   An undefended computer on the *internet* that is trying to attract *hackers*, *viruses*, *worms* and *spam*, so that their characteristics can be identified and defences designed and issued.

hot fixes   Vendor-generated software packages composed of one or more files that address an identified problem or *vulnerability*.

HotSpot   A wireless *access point* that, unless it is secure (that is, it is open), is accessible to any member of the public with a *wireless*-enabled PC – whether or not it is intended for public use. If the HotSpot is secure, then the *user* will need to know its *WEP* or *WPA key* to connect to it.

HTML   Hyper Text Markup Language – a computer language widely used to format web pages and e-mail and which is often also used for *spam*.

HTTP   Hypertext Transfer Protocol – the *protocol* for moving hypertext files across the *internet*, this is the standard language that computers use to communicate across the web.

HTTPS   This is a secure version of *HTTP*, using *SSL*.

Human Rights Act (HRA)   See Chapter 9.

identity management   This is the management of multiple versions of *user* identities across multiple *applications*, and might typically involve *single sign-on*, *password* synchronization, etc.

identity theft (SR) This is when someone gathers enough *information* about someone else (name, address, data of birth, *credit card* numbers, social security number, etc) to successfully impersonate that person online, by mail, over the telephone, or in person.

IE See *Internet Explorer*.

IEEE Institute of Electrical and Electronics Engineers.

IIS Internet Information Server – an original *Microsoft server operating system*, which has been replaced, and which was inadequately robust.

IMEI number The International Mobile Equipment Identity number is a 15-digit unique code that is used to identify a telephone to a *network*. It can (on most phones) be displayed by typing: *#06# on the keypad. It may also be printed on the compliance plate under the battery. When a phone is switched on, the IMEI is transmitted and automatically checked against the network's list of *blacklisted* phones in its EIR (Equipment ID Register) to establish whether or not the phone should be able to logon to the network and make calls.

impact The likely outcome of the successful exploitation of a *vulnerability* by a *threat*.

impact analysis Analysis and a financial evaluation of the likely outcome of the successful exploitation of a *vulnerability* by a *threat*, considering the *asset's availability, confidentiality* or *integrity*.

incident A single or a series of unwanted or unexpected *events* that have a significant probability of compromising business operations and threatening *information security**.

incident management (KC) This is the process of managing *incidents*; it usually depends on a pre-rehearsed plan and a set of tested options. See Chapter 4, rule 10.

information The *New Shorter Oxford English Dictionary 1993* provides these helpful definitions: 'knowledge or facts communicated about a particular subject, *events*, etc; intelligence, news', and, 'without necessary relation to a recipient: that which inheres in or is represented by a particular arrangement, sequence or set, that may be stored in, transferred by, and responded to by inanimate things'. Clearly *information*, or data, exists in many forms but, for the purposes of its security, we are concerned with data that has a *digital*, paper, or voice format.

information classification See *classification system*.

Information Commissioner See Chapter 9.

information processing facilities Any information processing *system, service of infrastructure*, or the physical location housing them*.

information security Preservation of the *confidentiality, integrity* and *availability* of *information*; in addition, other properties, such as *authenticity, accountability, non-repudiation* and *reliability* can also be involved*.

Information Security Management System (KC) (ISMS) That part of the overall management system, based on a business risk approach, to establish, implement, operate, monitor, review, maintain and improve *information security***.

information security policy (KC)   This is the organizational *policy* for securing its *information assets*. See Chapter 4, rule 1.

Infosec Basics for Business (KC)   The 14 essential, basic components of an organizational approach to *information security* – see Chapters 2 and 4.

infowar   See *cyber war*.

infrared   This is a communication method that uses the infrared spectrum in light beams. It is used in most TV remote systems and is also used to connect some *peripheral* devices (mice, keyboards) to computers.

infrastructure mode   A *WLAN* architecture in which a *wireless AP* provides the bridge between wireless *clients* and the fixed, existing *network*.

instant messaging   A communication methodology that is analogous to a private *chat room*; it enables you to communicate over the *internet* in real time with another person, using text.

insurance (KC)   Computers should be covered under insurance policies. Individuals and organizations both need to ensure that their insurance policies do specifically cover their various *information assets* and that the nature of the cover is adequate. See Chapter 4.

integrity   Safeguarding the accuracy and completeness of *information* and processing methods**.

intellectual property rights (or IPR)   See Chapter 9.

internet   The massive, global network of *networks*, connecting millions of computers, allowing any computer to communicate with any other by any one of a number of *protocols*. The internet is not the *web*.

internet cafes   These are cafes that provide banks of computers and *internet access*, for a fee, as well as refreshments.

Internet Explorer (IE)   *Microsoft's browser*.

Internet Highway Code (KC)   The 10 basic rules for SOHO (small office/home office) micro *networks* – see Chapters 2 and 3.

Internet Protocol (IP) **address**   Each computer connected to the web (or permanently connected to an individual *network*) has its own unique 32-*bit* address. This is written in *digital* form and translated into a *domain name* for ease of use. A *dial-up* connection usually works with dynamic address allocation from a pool of available addresses, so a user's *IP* address will be different at every *internet* logon. A *broadband* connection that is always on will have an unchanging address, which will offer more of a target for a *hacker*.

internet protocol security (IPSec)   Creates a secured connection between two *systems*. It defines how interoperable, secure host-to-host and client-to-host connections (known as *Virtual Private Networks*, or VPNs) are to work, creating an encrypted tunnel over a public *network*, which provides *privacy* as good as that available on a private network. See http://www.ietf.org for technical information.

Internet Storm Center The SANS institute's early warning centre for detecting rising *internet threats* is at http://isc.sans.org.

intranet That part of an organization's internal *network* that has the same functionality as the *internet*, consists of one or more web *servers*, and carries organization-specific information to which only authorized *users* have *access*. An intranet is not accessible to unauthorized users or web surfers.

intrusion An attempt to break into or misuse an *information processing system*, or bypass its *security controls*, in order to compromise the *confidentiality*, *integrity* and *availability* of *information* stored on it.

intrusion detection A (*network*) intrusion detection *system* is hardware or software that automates the process of monitoring *events* in systems or *networks* to detect *intrusions*. There are different types of intrusion detection systems. A (N)IDS, also known as a 'network sniffer', monitors *packets* on the network and attempts to discover if a *hacker* is attempting to break into the system (or cause a *denial of service attack*). A system integrity verifier (SIV) monitors system files to find when an intruder changes them so as to set up a *back door*. *Log file* monitors (LFM) monitor log files generated by network services. In a similar manner to (N)IDS, these systems look for patterns in the log files that suggest an intruder is attacking.

IP Internet Protocol – the most basic *protocol* for communicating on the *internet*.

IP address See *Internet Protocol address* and *domain name*.

IPSec See *internet protocol security*.

IP spoofing See *spoofing*.

IrDA The Infrared Data Association's standard for digital infrared connectivity.

ISBS Information Security Breaches Survey – carried out bi-annually by PriceWaterhouseCoopers for the UK's DTI.

ISMS See *Information Security Management System*.

ISO 17799:2005 (KC) The international code of best practice for *information security* and, specifically, the revised version issued in 2005; see '*IT Governance: A Manager's Guide to Data Security and BS 7799/ISO 17799*'.

ISP Internet Service Provider.

IT governance (KC) A framework for the leadership, organizational structures and business processes, standards and compliance to these standards, which ensures that the organization's IT supports and enables the achievement of its strategies and objectives. See Chapter 6.

Java A programming language from Sun Microsystems that was designed for writing programs (*applets*) that include animations, scrolling text, sound effects, games, etc, that can be downloaded from the web without fear of *viruses* or other harm to your computer.

JavaScript   A scripting language widely used to create *pop-up* and pop-down ads, and other functionality, on web pages.

JPEGs   Joint Photographics Experts Group – a compression technique for colour images and photographs and, therefore, how they are saved. There is a future possibility that JPEG *viruses* might emerge; these are best resisted by doing the basics consistently.

junk mail   See *spam*.

Kerberos   Available free from MIT, this is a *network user authentication* system based on *key* distribution (and can be embedded in virtually any other network *protocol*) that works on both fixed and *wireless* networks.

key   The value used, in conjunction with an algorithm, to encrypt or decrypt data. A key may be either public (see *PKI)* or private.

keystroke logger (SR)   Software that records *key* depressions on a computer keyboard; the software can either be installed on the computer (in which case it can be detected by *anti-spyware* software) or it can run inside a secret device attached to the computer, in which case anti-spyware software will not detect it.

LAN   Local Area Network; two or more computers connected, either physically or *wirelessly*, and able to share resources.

layered security (KC)   Multiple layers of security technology and administrative processes working together to provide a level of protection appropriate to the *asset* being protected; multiple barriers and inbuilt limits to possible damage form part of such a defence in depth. Larger organizations, in particular, need to deploy layered security *architectures*.

legislation   There's a lot of it, and there's an overview in Chapter 9.

licence   Any software that is being used is potentially subject to *copyright* restrictions and it is essential that the organization ensure that it has the correct type and number of licences for this software. There are two types of *user* licence. The first is known as a 'per seat' licence, the second is for 'concurrent users'. Per seat requires there to be a licence for every installation, or instance, of the software; typically, Microsoft Office licences, for instance, are supplied on this basis. Concurrent user allows for a maximum number of simultaneous users and is more normal for shared software, such as some database *applications*. This enables the *client* software to be installed on many machines, but typically the *server* software is set so that it will not allow more than the licensed number of users to work simultaneously. See Chapter 4, rule 3.

Linux   *Open source* software, originally aimed at desktop workstations.

log files   Files that contain logs of specific activity types.

logical   Objects and methods that are apparent to *users* and/or *applications*, as opposed to the physical objects and methods upon which they are based; you have to have physical *access* to a computer before you can have *logical* access to its folders.

MAC See *Media Access Control*.

macro virus (SR) A *virus* that spreads through the macro-scripting language used in Microsoft Office *applications*.

mail server The server that provides central support for mail *clients*.

malware (SR) Any form of 'malicious stuff' that tries to clog up your computer. It includes *adware, spam, spim, spyware, viruses, worms, Trojans* and automated *exploits*. Its attack *vectors* include e-mail attachments, *instant messaging*, unprotected *internet* connections and *browsers*. See *scumware*.

man in the middle (SR) A hacker places him or herself undetected between two parties to an *internet* transaction, whether on a *LAN*, an unsecured internet link, a *WLAN* or on a cellular telephone network. The hacker intercepts and reads messages between the two parties and can alter them without the intended recipient knowing what has happened. This is often recognized as a form of *masquerading*; see also *evil twin*.

masquerading (SR) A hacker will pretend to be a legitimate *user*, trying to access legitimate information, using a *password* or *PIN* that was easily obtained or copied, and will then try to access more confidential information or execute commands that are not usually publicly accessible. See also *evil twin*.

Mbps 'Megabits per second' is a measure for digital data transfer rates and a megabit in this context is 1 million *bits*. In the context of data storage, a megabit is 1,024 kilobits.

Media Access Control Every *WiFi* device has a unique *MAC* number allocated by its manufacturer. A *wireless AP* can be programmed to accept only certain MAC addresses and to block all others. While this is relatively simple for a *SoHo network*, it can be time-consuming to set up and maintain in a large corporate network. It is also possible for a *hacker* to *spoof* a MAC address.

Microsoft Creator of NT4, Win 2000, Office, Explorer, XP, Server2003 etc.

mobile code Programs that are sent in one version only to a heterogeneous collection of processors and are executed with the same semantic on each of those processors without explicit installation or execution by the recipient*.

mobile phones Surely everyone knows what these are?

mobile worker This is someone who doesn't work from a fixed geographic location and whose job requires them to spend a substantial amount of time out of the office, 'on the road,' or travelling. Mobile workers use laptops (increasingly connecting through *wireless HotSpots*), *cellphones* and *PDAs* to keep in touch with their offices and homes.

modem Modulator/**de-m**odulator – a device that enables a computer to transmit data over *analogue* telephone lines.

MPEG Moving Pictures Experts Group – a standard for *digital* video and audio compression.

MSN Messenger   *Microsoft's instant messaging* service.

multiple sign-on   A *user* within an organization who is authorized to use multiple *applications* and services would have to sign-on individually to each one, unless the organization deploys *single sign-on* software.

NDA (KC)   Non-disclosure agreement – legal agreement that sets out the specific terms on which one party will share confidential *information* with another; it includes an agreement by the second party not to disclose or otherwise use any of the *information* made available under the terms of the NDA. See Chapter 4, rule 4.

netspionage (SR)   Corporate espionage, carried out online.

network   A number of computers (at least two) linked together, either with or without central *servers*.

network monitoring   This is also known as 'sniffing' and involves deploying some code on the *internet* to monitor all traffic in order to look for *passwords*. These, and other ostensibly confidential information, are often sent across the internet 'in the clear' and, therefore, can easily be located and written to the *hacker's* workstation for future use. When this technique is used to try to detect hacker activity, it is called *intrusion detection*.

network perimeter   See *perimeter*.

network sniffer   See *intrusion detection*.

non-disclosure agreement   See *NDA*.

non-repudiation (KC)   A cryptographic method of providing the sender of data with proof of delivery and assuring the recipient of the sender's identity, so that neither can later deny that the data was transmitted. This is critical in *e-commerce* – see Chapter 8.

online payment service   A number of organizations offer *third-party* payment services. The best known are: WorldPay, PayPal, Amazon.com Payments, Yahoo! PayDirect, and VeriSign Inc.

open source   Software whose code is open for anyone to look at and modify. *Linux* is a well-known type of open source software. See www.opensource.org.

operating system (OS)   The OS is the software that controls how a computer uses its memory, disk space, folders and files, desktop, etc. *Microsoft* Windows and Apple Macintosh are the two most popular proprietary operating systems. There are also *open source* operating systems.

opt in   An option in marketing campaigns that enables individuals to explicitly consent to participate now or in future.

opt out   An option in marketing campaigns that enables individuals to explicitly decline to participate now or in future

OS   See *operating system*.

Outlook   The *Microsoft* e-mail *client*.

Outlook Express   The cut-down version of *Outlook,* designed for home *users*.

OWASP   The **O**pen **W**eb **A**pplication **S**ecurity **P**roject (www.owasp.org) specifies the top ten *application* vulnerabilities that an organization should secure.

packets   These are the standard unit(s) for data sent across the *internet*. Data is broken up into packets, which allows multiple transmissions to share the same line, and they are routed back together again at the destination and are placed back in their original order.

PAP   Password Authentication Protocol – this is a login security protocol that is less secure than *CHAP* because the *password* is sent to the *client* as clear text.

parental control (KC)   This is software that is designed to enable parents to scan, *filter* and *control* the websites visited by their children, to protect them from objectionable content. See the *Internet Highway Code* in Chapter 3.

password (KC)   A string of characters entered to a computer, an *application* or a *network* by a *user* to verify their identity as the owner of a specific *user name*.

password cracking (SR)   On balance, very easy. Most *users* do not set up *password*s or, if they do, they use very simple passwords that they can easily remember, like 'secret' or 'password', or their children's names, or birthdays, sports teams, or particular anniversaries, or family names. While some *hackers* can quickly identify particular users' passwords, software is now available on the *internet* that will apply *brute force* to automatically, and at high speed, try every theoretically possible alphanumeric combination of *user name* and password and, usually aided by a dictionary (a *dictionary attack*) of common passwords, this can quickly enable a hacker to gain *access* to a *system*. Once a hacker locates the list of encrypted user passwords on the security *server*, he or she can use internet-available software tools to decrypt it. See Chapter 4, rule 7.

patch   An update to a file that replaces only parts of the file, rather than the whole file.

payload   The damage or other malicious activity that a *virus*, *worm* or *spam* causes.

PCI Data Security Standard   The Payment Card Industry Data Security Standard, V1.0 of which was published in December 2004, sets out 12 information security requirements that apply to all organizations involved in processing credit card data or transactions of any sort. The requirements range from the technical level ('assign a unique ID') to the strategic ('protect stored data'). See www.itgovernance.co.uk/page.current_issues for a copy of the Standard.

PDA A Personal Digital Assistant is a device that stores *digital* contact, diary and other data; it may also store e-mail and be capable of communicating (either wired or wirelessly) with a computer or a *network*. A *Blackberry* is a form of *PDA* that has *mobile phone* connectivity and exists specifically to handle e-mail while on the move.

Pdf Portable Document Format – a file extension indicating that a document has been saved in Adobe's proprietary format.

peer-to-peer A network connecting two or more computers directly to one another, without using a central file *server*.

penetration testing (KC) This is the organized process of assessing the full range of *threats* to an organization and setting out deliberately to infiltrate and penetrate its *systems*, using any and all methods, from technological hacking through to *social engineering*.

perimeter The organization's boundary has both physical and *logical* aspects. In *information security* terms, the perimeter is where you draw the line, the line behind which only authorized and authenticated *users* may go. In today's business environment, that perimeter is increasingly a mobile one.

personal data That *information* about a living person (that is, not an organization) that is protected by *legislation* and regulation – see *Data Protection Act* in Chapter 9.

Personal Digital Assistants See *PDAs*.

PGP Pretty Good Privacy – a *public key encryption* program that enables files or messages to be exchanged with confidentiality and *authentication*.

phishing Sending e-mails that falsely claim to come from a legitimate company in an attempt to scam *users* into surrendering *information* that can be used for *identity theft*.

physical security (KC) This is security that is effective in the *analogue* world. See Chapter 4, rule 5.

PIN Personal Identity Number.

PKI Public Key Infrastructure; the combination of standards, *protocols* and software that supports *public key encryption*.

platform A hardware and software combination (for example, Windows XP on an Intel PC).

policy (KC) Overall intention and direction as formally expressed by management*. See Chapter 4, rule 1.

pop ups and **pop downs** Small windows that appear when *users* visit some websites, pop ups are the windows that pop up, pop downs do it in the other direction.

ports Hardware ports are connection points for cables, and *logical* (or virtual) ports are *access points* for *protocol*.

PowerPoint *Microsoft*'s slide presentation *application*.

printers Devices for printing *digital information* onto *analogue* paper.

privacy The control that individuals have over the collection, use and distribution of their personal, private information – see also Chapter 9.

Privacy and Electronic Communications Regulations 2003 – see Chapter 9.

private key One of two *keys* used in *public key encryption* (PKI). This key is kept private and secret, and used to encrypt data prior to transmission or to decrypt data that has been encrypted with the corresponding *public key*.

privilege A privilege is any facility in a multi-user *system* that enables one *user* to override system or *application controls*. Inadequate *control* of privileges invariably leads to their inappropriate use; equally invariably, this abuse leads to system security breaches and is a major contributory factor in system failures. The most critical privileges are those that enable *system administrators* to do their jobs.

procedure A set of specific, sequential steps.

process A series of related activities.

project governance The framework and rules for controlling how project decisions are made and project activity monitored.

protocol A set of rules that govern an activity or process.

proxy server This is a *server* that sits between a *client* (for example, a *browser*) and real server, or between an organization and the *internet*. It improves performance by filling a request directly rather than forwarding the *user* to the internet if the necessary information is available. Proxy servers can also block unauthorized activity – outgoing or incoming (*firewall*).

p2p See *peer-to-peer*.

public key One of two *keys* used in *public key encryption* (PKI). The public key is released to the public, and used to encrypt data prior to transmission to the holder of the *private key* or to *decrypt* data that has been encrypted with the corresponding private key. It can also be used to verify the user's *digital signature*.

public key encryption See *asymmetric encryption*.

public terminals Computer terminals that are in a public area, and designed for *access* by non-specific *users*.

RADIUS Remote Authentication Dial-In User Service is a *protocol* for administering and securing *remote access* to a *network*. It needs an *authentication server*, *client* protocols and an accounting *server*, all of which can be mounted on a single machine. The RADIUS authentication server validates the *user* credentials (*user name* and *password*) before allowing *access*. It can provide different levels of *user privileges*. It does not provide *encryption*.

reboot This is what you have to do after your computer has *crash*ed.

recovery This is what you have to bring about after an *incident* that interrupts *business continuity* – a *system* failure may mean that data is lost and has to be recovered from the *backup* tapes.

recycle bin The *Microsoft* desktop folder into which deletions go – and stay, until you remember to go and empty the deleted items folder. Until you empty this folder, any files in it can be dragged back into use.

Regulation of Investigatory Powers Act (RIPA) See Chapter 9.

reliability Minimal maintenance, minimal manpower requirements, maximum *resilience*.

remote access This is *system access* by a *remote user*.

remote control software Software that a *remote user* deploys via a remote *access port* to control a computer.

remote user A *user* who is not within the organizational *perimeter*, and is the general category to which *teleworkers* and *mobile workers* belong. Remote *users* can also be technicians who need to *access server* software to carry out repairs or maintenance; they could also do other things, as could anyone else who finds the *remote access port*.

reputation damage This is what can happen when *information* about serious *information security incident*s gets into the public domain. It can be very costly for individuals and for organizations.

resilience The ability to bounce back when attacked.

retrovirus (SR) A *virus* that attempts to disable *anti-virus software*.

risk Combination of the probability of an *event* and its consequence*.

risk analysis Systematic use of *information* to identify sources and to estimate the risk*.

risk appetite An organization's overall attitude to *risk*, the balance between risk and return and the trade-off between security and flexibility, usually a strategic preference expressed by the organization's board.

risk assessment Overall process of *risk analysis* and *risk evaluation**.

risk classification The classification of a *risk* as low, medium or high depending on the *risk assessment*.

risk evaluation Process of comparing the estimated risk against given risk criteria to determine the significance of the *risk**.

risk log This is produced through a *risk analysis* process and is the tabular list of all the organization's *assets*, together with their *threats*, vulnerabilities, *impacts*, probabilities and *risk classification*. The risk log should include all the *information assets* of the organization.

risk management Coordinated activities to direct and *control* an organization with respect to *risk* (and usually includes *risk assessment*, *risk treatment*, risk acceptance and risk communication)*.

risk treatment Process of selection and implementation of measures to modify *risk**.

risk treatment plan The overall plan for *risk treatment*, reflecting the corporate *risk appetite*.

router A device that connects a number of computers together or to the *internet*.

safe harbour See Chapter 9.

SANS The SANS Institute – www.sans.org – was established in 1989 and many of its resources are free to *users*. It is 'by far the largest source for *information security* training and *certification* in the world. It also develops, maintains, and makes available at no cost, the largest collection of research documents about various aspects of *information security*, and it operates the *internet*'s early warning system – the *Internet Storm Center'*.

SANS top 20 A list of the 20 most important vulnerabilities in current software, that should help organizations prioritize their patching activity. See also *CVE* and *Bugtraq*.

Sarbanes Oxley (SOX) See Chapter 9 and, more importantly, *IT Governance: A Manager's Guide to Data Security and BS 7799/ISO 17799*.

screensaver A program that displays an image (blank or moving) on a computer screen after the computer has had no input for a period of time – originally designed so that images wouldn't be burned into old CRT screens, they have become entertaining.

script kiddie (SR) Not as sophisticated as a *hacker* and so hasn't yet qualified for a hat but, using their own very simple code or, more usually, programs found on the *internet*, they can be just as lethal to unprotected systems as real hackers. Quite often, script kiddies are found in IT departments where their interest in testing the systems they are employed to protect can take them beyond the law.

scumware See *malware*.

Search Engine Optimization (SEO) The process of making website content more search engine friendly to make the website rank higher in web searches.

Secure Electronic Transaction (SET) A *protocol*, developed jointly by Visa and Mastercard, for enabling secure, cost-effective bank and *credit card* transactions over open *networks*. SET includes protocols for purchasing goods and services electronically, for authorizing payments, and for requesting and obtaining *digital certificates*.

secure HTTP See *HTTPS*.

Secure Sockets Layer (KC) (SSL) A handshake *protocol* that provides *security* and *privacy* to *internet* transactions. It is *application* independent; after an SSL session starts, other *protocols* (like *HTTP* and FTP) can be layered transparently on top of it. It has become one of the most popular security protocols on the *internet*. Installation of a *server* ID, or *digital certificate*, will automatically activate SSL on the server and this enables that website to communicate securely with any visiting *browser*. *Client* and vendor servers are able to authenticate one another automatically. Once this is complete, SSL will encrypt all communication (data such as *credit* *card* numbers and other personal information) between the web server and the visiting browser with a unique session *key*. The session key is not used again. SSL was designed to ensure that, even if *information* is intercepted, it cannot be viewed by someone who is not authorized to do so. The default settings in browsers should identify sites that are not secure and should warn that information submitted could be intercepted or observed by a *third party*. This warning does not appear where there is a valid SSL connection. There are other signs that there is an SSL connection: the *URL* will change from http to *https* and a closed padlock will appear in the bar at the bottom of the browser window. See Chapter 8, on *e-commerce*.

security What you get when you have secured something.

security centre (KC) (Windows XP SP2) This is the single control point for the Windows *internet* security features, from which the *firewall*, *anti-virus software*, *automatic update* service and internet options can be controlled. It can be accessed through the *Control Panel*.

server A computer on a *network* that stores shared *information* or which handles common tasks for a number of *client* computers.

server farm (also, server cluster) A collection of networked, load-balanced *servers* in a single secure site that are capable of accomplishing more than a single server through task distribution – which also helps provide operational redundancy *backup*.

service packs The cumulative product and security software updates (usually including all previous *hot fixes*, security updates and *patches*) which need to be downloaded from the supplier's website in order to keep the product up to date.

SET See *Secure Electronic Transaction*.

shareware Software that is provided on the basis that, if the user likes it, the *user* will pay something for it. You can share this software with friends, but they too are expected to make a contribution.

single sign-on (or SSO) A means of passing *user* credentials between *applications* without the user having to authenticate each time they seek to use another application for which they are authorized.

smart cards Credit-card-sized devices that have an embedded chip containing a small amount of data that, together with an access code or PIN, enables a *user* to be authenticated. Smart cards can store *digital certificates*, *private keys*, *public keys* and *passwords*.

smart phones Mobile phones that combine mobile phone functionality with that of a *PDA*; the *user* can talk to others, send and receive text and voice messages as well as send and receive e-mail, store calendar information and other data.

smart token A *USB* device that contains a computer chip that securely stores *information* about *user*s and supports *authentication*, *digital signatures* and *biometrics*; when used in conjunction with a strong *password*, they make possible *two factor authentication*.

S/MIME Multipurpose Internet Mail Extensions (MIME) is a specification that provides a standard method for attaching to basic e-mail messages additional files such as pictures, audio and *application* files. Secure MIME adds security features such as *digital signatures* and *encryption* services to the basic MIME specification, thus protecting the privacy of e-mail and its attachments.

snarfing See *bluesnarfing*.

SoA See *Statement of Applicability*.

social engineering (SR) The easiest and most common method of gaining access to a *network*, tricking someone into providing confidential *information*. The *hacker*, for instance, poses as a network *administrator* or a fellow employee, with an urgent problem, which can only be resolved by the employee providing confidential information (such as *user name* or *password*). Alternatively, the hacker has a false business card, claiming to be a key technical or business support representative, or claims to be a new employee trying to get up to speed in the business. Passwords should NEVER be divulged to anyone, anywhere, for any reason, under any conditions. NOT EVER. This is one of the most important, fundamental and basic security rules.

SOHO Small Office, Home Office.

SOX See *Sarbanes Oxley*, in Chapter 9.

SPAM (SR) Unsolicited commercial bulk e-mail, or *junk mail*.

SPIM (SR) *Spam* sent through an instant message.

spoofing (SR) IP spoofing gains unauthorized *access* to a *system* by *masquerading* as a valid *internet protocol* (*IP*) *address*. Web spoofing involves the *hacker* re-directing traffic from a valid web address to a fraudulent, look-alike website where customer *information* (and particularly *credit card* information) is captured for later illegal reuse – see also *phishing*.

spyware (SR) Any software that, without your explicit consent, shares information about you with a *third party* on the *internet*.

SSID Service Set Identifier – the name that uniquely identifies a *LAN*. *Wireless* devices need to know the SSID of a *WLAN* before they can connect to it.

SSL See *Secure Sockets Layer*.

SSL VPN See *Secure Sockets Layer* and *Virtual Private Network*.

Statement of Applicability (KC) (SoA) Document describing the *control* objectives and controls that are relevant and applicable to the organization's *ISMS*, based on the results and conclusions of the *risk assessment* and *risk treatment* processes**.

steganography Or *digital watermarking*, a method of hiding *information* in other data, such as voice communications, visual images and music, in order to provide *forensic* evidence of *copyright* ownership and trace the source of infringing material.

strong authentication See *two factor authentication*.

surf control This is a software technology that is designed to allow blocking to surfers of particular sites, or groups of sites. Parents can use it to protect their children from offensive or dangerous sites, and organizations can use it to deter their employees from visiting illegal or undesirable sites, or doing other undesirable things. Different *filters* and different environments mean that different packages are deployed for each type of control. In the United Kingdom, organizations should only deploy surf control technology in the workplace in conjunction with an *acceptable use policy*.

symmetric 'Correspondence of parts'.

symmetric encryption Uses same *key* (or code) to encrypt and decrypt *information* – see also *DES* and *asymmetric encryption*.

system Any combination of hardware and software used for processing *information*, and which has a data entry point and a data exit point. A system consists of a number of components. A single data *asset* (such as a file, whether electronic or paper) is a component of a system.

system access controls (KC) Controls that restrict *access* to *information processing systems* through a combination of *guidelines* and technological security measures that implement those guidelines. See Chapter 4, rule 8.

System utilities A software program that will perform a specific task, usually related to managing system resources.

TACACS+ Terminal Access Controller Access Control System + – an authentication protocol that has replaced and is not compatible with TACACS.

TCP/IP model Transmission Control Protocol/Internet Protocol – this is a suite of communications *protocols* used to connect host computers on the *internet*. TCP/IP is the de facto standard for transmitting *information* over *networks*.

telecommunications regulations See Chapter 9.

teleworker This is someone who works primarily from home. The description originated with the idea that someone who didn't physically need to be in the office could work from home and keep in touch when necessary by telephone. Nowadays, a teleworker is likely to need a fully set up electronic home office, including a workstation, multipurpose *printer*/copier/scanner, *broadband internet* connection, fax machine, wrist rests, screen guards and so on.

terminal The screen and input device through which a computer system can be accessed.

third party A person or body recognized as being independent of the parties involved in a particular process or operation or business.

threat A potential cause of an unwanted *incident*, which may result in harm to a system or organization*.

Thunderbird An *open source* e-mail *client* from the Mozilla foundation.

TickIt An ISO 9000 compliant standard for software development processes.

TKIP The Temporal **K**ey **I**ntegrity **P**rotocol is a data-confidentiality *protocol* that was designed to improve the security of legacy products running *WEP*.

Trojan (SR) A Trojan is hostile code concealed within and purporting to be bona fide code. It is designed to reach a target stealthily and be executed inadvertently. It may have been installed at the time the software was developed. They can be programs that, while perhaps appearing to be a useful utility, are designed to secretly damage the host system. Some will also try to open up host systems to outside attack.

trusted Securely configured and therefore not expected to be the source of malicious activity – see also *untrusted*.

two-factor authentication *Authentication* that requires two different methods (for example, a *smart card* or *biometrics* plus a *password*) of identifying a *user*, both of which must match the credentials set up in the system for that *user*.

untrusted Not *trusted* – a device (usually) that is not – or cannot be assumed to be – securely configured and not subject to malicious action.

update 'A broadly released fix for a specific problem addressing a non-critical, non-security-related bug' – *Microsoft*. Some updates are critical, though.

update services See *automatic updates*.

upgrade Newer versions of an already installed software package; the *upgrade* process should leave existing data and *user* preferences intact while replacing the existing software with a newer version.

UPS (KC) **U**ninterruptible **P**ower **S**ource – this is a device that is designed to keep other electrically powered devices operating when the normal power supply fails. A UPS should, at the very least, be rated as capable of meeting the power requirements of the device(s) it is supporting for long enough to allow an orderly shutdown of the services. The length of time required for this may need to be ascertained by testing. See Chapter 4, rule 11.

URL **U**niform **R**esource **L**ocator, the address of a website on the world wide web.

USB **U**niversal **S**erial **B**us – a computer standard designed to eliminate the guesswork in connecting peripherals to computers.

USB stick (or **flash card**) A portable memory device with a *USB*.

user An individual, automated process or system that has *access* rights to a specified system.

user agreement (KC) This is the formal, standard document that all new *users* should be required to sign before they are issued their *user name*.

This agreement should describe their *access rights* and should set out the organization's requirements around *system* use and *password* choice and protection. See Chapter 4, rule 7.

user IDs   See *user name*.

user name (KC)   Every *user* should have a specific and unique name for use on the *system*; this name should be created and allocated in line with a standard procedure and should be set up on the system with specific *access rights* and *privileges*. The user name has to be created before the user can *access* the system for the first time. See Chapter 4, rule 7.

user rights   The specific *application access rights* associated with a specific *user name*.

VAR   Value-added reseller.

vector   In computing, this is the method that *malware* uses to propagate itself, or through which it attacks its targets.

Virtual Private Networks (KC) (SSL, IPSEC)   Encrypted and authenticated *logical* (not physical) links across shared or public *networks* that are used to provide remote links to an organizational network. A VPN *server* within the organizational *perimeter* encrypts data sent to a VPN client outside the perimeter, and vice versa.

virus (SR)   A virus is a piece of computer code that is designed to make your computer sick. Like biological viruses, it indiscriminately selects and infects those whose defences are weak or non-existent. Technically, a virus has at least two properties: it is a program capable of replicating, that is, producing functional copies of itself, and it depends on a host file (a document or executable file, shared by e-mail or *instant messaging*) to carry each copy. It may or may not have a '*payload*', the ability to do something funny or destructive or clever when it arrives:

- There are some 100,000 known viruses in the *wild*. These range from primitive bits of code written at the dawn of computing time, and from which almost all computers are now completely immune, to more destructive creatures like 2004's MyDoom, Slammer, Sobig (with all its variants) and Bugbear. Up-to-date *anti-virus* software protects against all of these, without you ever having to know what they do or how they work.
- Viruses exploit software faults (vulnerabilities) to attack computers and their *payload*s range from silly messages to individual *key*s becoming inoperative to the complete death of your computer.
- The same virus doesn't always have the same name with every *anti-virus* vendor. This is very irritating and it reflects the fact that the same virus is usually discovered, analysed, reverse engineered and the appropriate anti-virus signature update produced by a number of

competitive vendors working in parallel, each of them having allocated the virus their own version of the name.

▪ Most viruses attack *Microsoft* products, not just because Microsoft
products are full of flaws (vulnerabilities) but because it is the most
widely used computer software in the world, installed on in excess of
90 per cent of desktops. Computer viruses spread by harvesting e-
mail address books and forwarding themselves to everyone you know
– in an e-mail that is identified as having come from you – a good
way of losing friends and business contacts.

▪ It's not just Microsoft, though. ALL software has vulnerabilities, even
the *open source* versions. Visit *Bugtraq* or *CVE* to get a techies-eye view
of the range of software vulnerabilities that can be exploited by virus
and *worm* writers.

▪ And it's not just workstations and computer networks that have virus
challenges: increasingly, *PDAs* and *cellphones* are coming under attack
and, as they too need to connect to the corporate *network*, they too
need to be protected.

▪ *Virus writers* intend to exploit vulnerabilities in their target software
and, as soon as a weakness is identified, the race is on to exploit it –
and to see the attack off. The speed with which new viruses are developed is increasing – it is now only a matter of days between the
announcement of a *vulnerability* and the appearance of the first virus
exploiting it.

virus hoax   There are people out there who think it's dead funny to send
e-mails to everyone they know, warning of a virus that isn't one. Frankly,
if a real or important new virus existed that you had to hear about from
some acquaintance rather than from your *anti-virus* company, you've either
chosen a very poor anti-virus supplier (if you have one at all) or you're
being hoaxed. If you're reading this book, chances are it'll be the latter.
http://vmyths.com/index.cfm is a good place to go if you really want to
be sure that a message you've received is a hoax.

virus writers   'People' who write viruses; they should be taken outside
and have unspeakable things done to them. Mostly, they are sad people
who do it for fun and because they enjoy the challenge of writing clever
code. Sometimes they do it out of loneliness, or because they want to have
some impact on the world. They often work together and have online
groups, websites and communities through which they share work and
ideas. They also compete with one another and certainly their relationship
with *anti-virus* companies is often extremely hostile. Virus toolkits are
available online, so that anyone with limited code writing skills can also
create a virus.

VoIP/VOB   Voice over *IP*/Voice over *Broadband* is a technology that enables voice-to-voice communication across the *internet*.

VPN See *Virtual Private Network*.

vulnerability   A weakness of an *asset* or group of assets that can be exploited by a *threat**. There are regularly updated central stores of known vulnerabilities at *Bugtraq* and *CVE* and in the *SANS top 20*.

vulnerability assessment   This is the (usually automated) evaluation (or *vulnerability scanning*) of *operating systems* and *applications* to identify missing fixes for known problems so that the necessary fixes can be installed and the *systems* made safe.

vulnerability scanning (KC)   An automated process of scanning a *network* or a series of *information assets* to establish if they display any of the characteristics of known vulnerabilities. *See* Chapter 4, rule 9.

WAN   See *Wide Area Network*.

war chalking   The (Great Depression era, hobo-style) practice of using chalk to physically mark '*HotSpots*' from which (usually) unauthorized *access* to nearby *wireless networks* can be achieved. This has now been largely superseded by *internet*-based location lists of available unsecured (open) wireless networks – see www.wifinder.com and www.wardrive. net/general/hotspots for instance.

war dialling (SR)   A computer program (usually *freeware* or *shareware*) used by *hackers* to identify phone numbers that can connect to a computer *modem*. The program automatically dials a defined range of phone numbers and records in a database those numbers that connect successfully. Some programs can also identify the computer's *OS* and may also conduct automated *penetration testing* by running through a predetermined list of common *user names* and *passwords* in an attempt to gain *access* to the *system*.

war driving (SR)   The practice of driving around business or residential areas, scanning for *wireless networks*. Any computer that is wireless enabled can be used for this purpose, although there are a number of software tools and peripherals that substantially improve the speed, accuracy and covertness of this activity. Netstumbler is a well-known war driving kit; at less than £60, it comes complete with a discreet, omni-directional antennae fitted on a magnetic base.

web   See *world wide web*.

webmail   An e-mail service that sits on a web server and is accessible through a *browser*.

Webmaster   The person, in an organization, who is responsible for the *configuration* and maintenance of the organization's web *servers* and web presence.

WEP   Wired Equivalent Privacy is a *protocol* in the *IEEE*'s original *802.11* standard for *wireless networking* that was designed to tackle the *vulnerability* that comes from data sharing radio waves. It has many flaws and should not be relied on to provide adequate security.

white hat A type of *hacker*.

whitelist The list of people that you positively want to receive e-mails from.

Wide Area Network A network of two or more *LANs*, connected either through physical links (leased lines or the telephone system) or satellites. The *internet* is the largest *WAN* in existence.

WiFi Wireless Fidelity – is the name given to *wireless* networking that meets a number of standards promulgated by the *IEEE*. Those most commonly encountered are *802.11a*, *802.11b* (the original WiFi), *802.11g* and *802.11i*.

WiFi Alliance This is an independent, non-profit organization that certifies *WiFi* product interoperability and operates the *WiFi Zone HotSpot* programme. Its website is at www.wi-fi.org.

WiFi certified Means that the produce has been certified by the *WiFi Alliance* to be interoperable with whichever *802.11* (usually a, b and g) *wireless* standards it claims.

WiFi Zone The *WiFi Alliance* operates a programme to identify and mark public *APs* with a standard logo, supported by a website that identifies, worldwide, the location of local *WiFi HotSpots*. This website is at www.wi-fizone.org; it can be accessed by WAP phone (on http://wap.wi-fizone.org) to easily identify a nearby, local WiFi Zone HotSpot.

wild This is the digital online world, the place where *viruses* and *worms* spread, beyond human control.

WiMax The next generation of *wireless* technology – with wireless ranges of up to 10 miles and *broadband* speeds – the first usable technology is due soon – see http://wimaxxed.com/.

wireless A communication method that does not rely on cabling of any sort – see *WiFi*.

wireless LAN A local area *network* consisting of a number of wireless clients accessing a fixed network (for example, an *internet* backbone) through a wireless *access point*.

WLAN See *wireless LAN*.

workstation A computer that has a mass storage device (*hard drive*) and a large, high resolution screen and uses an *operating system* that provides a graphical user interface (GUI).

world wide web This is an information sharing construct that sits on top of the *internet*, and uses *HTTP* to transmit data. Clearly, it is not synonymous with the internet. A *browser* is required for accessing web content.

worm (SR) Unlike a *virus*, a worm is autonomous. It does not rely upon a host file to carry it. It can replicate itself (that is, is self-propagating), which it does by means of a transmission medium such as e-mail, *instant messaging*, Internet Relay Chat, network connections, etc. Polymorphic worms are capable of evolving in the *wild*, so that they can more effectively overcome evolving virus defences.

WPA WiFi Protected Access – a more secure version of *802.11* that uses *TKIP*. Also see *802.11i*.

WPA2 The interoperable version of *WPA*.

XML Extensible Markup Language – a flexible method of creating common information formats and to share them across the web.

zero day exploits (SR) This is an exploit that takes advantage of a *vulnerability* on the same day that it is announced (or becomes generally known) – *anti-virus* companies and software manufacturers have zero days' grace in which to develop and launch a fix or a *patch*.

zombie (SR) This, as you might expect, is a once independent computer that is now under the discretionary, malign control of another computer somewhere else in the world. A *remote user* can take advantage of inadequate *anti-virus* and *firewall* defences to install *remote control software* on other computers. This remote control software enables the remote user to use your computer – without you even being aware of it – for the mass forwarding of *spam* or as part of a massive, coordinated attack on another website – a *distributed denial of service* attack. In the long run, the future of electronic communication depends on every computer being sufficiently well protected so that none can be used as zombies.

Appendix 1

Further reading

Adediran, Peter (2002), *Business, Law & the Internet – A Practical Guide*, Kogan Page, London

Allen, Julia (2001), *The CERT Guide to System and Network Security Practices*, Addison-Wesley, Boston

Andress, Mandy (2002), *Surviving Security*, Sams Publishing, Indianapolis

Bandyo-padhyay, Nanda (2001), *Computing for Non-Specialists*, Addison-Wesley, Boston

Beaver, Kevin (2004), *Hacking For Dummies*, Wiley Publishing Inc, Hoboken, NJ

Cobb, Chey (2003), *Network Security For Dummies*, Wiley Publishing Inc, Hoboken, NJ

Feinstein, Ken (2004), *Fight Spam, Viruses, Pop-Ups & Spyware*, McGraw Hill Osborne, New York

Fogie, Seth and Peikari, Cyrus (2002), *Windows Internet Security*, Prentice-Hall, Upper Saddle River, NJ

Furnell, Steven (2002), *Cybercrime*, Addison-Wesley, Boston

Gentry, Lorna (2002), *Technology Survival Guide*, Que Publishing, Indianapolis

Gralla, Preston (2002), *Internet Privacy and Security*, Alpha, Indianapolis

Holt, Jeremey and Newton, Jeremy (eds) (2004), *A Manager's Guide to IT Law*, BCS, Swindon

Jolly, Adam (2003), *Managing Business Risk: A Practical Guide to Protecting Your Business*, Kogan Page, London

Jolly, Adam (2005), *The Secure Online Business: E-commerce, IT Functionality & Business Continuity*, Kogan Page, London

Komar, Brian, Beekelarr, Ronald and Wettern, Joern (2003), *Firewalls For Dummies*, Wiley Publishing Inc, Hoboken, NJ

Krause, Micki and Tipton, Harold (2004), *Information Security Management Handbook*, Auerbach, Boca Raton, FL

Lewis, Barry D and Davis, Peter T (2004), *Wireless Networks for Dummies*, Wiley Publishing Inc, Hoboken, NJ

Lilley, Peter (2002), *Hacked, Attacked and Abused: Digital Crime Exposed*, Kogan Page, London

Sandhu, Roopendra Jeet (2002), *Disaster Recovery Planning*, Premier Press, Rocklin, CA

Schneier, Bruce (2000), *Secrets & Lies: Digital Security in a Networked World*, Wiley Computer Publishing, Hoboken, NJ

Appendix 2

Useful websites

Blogspot
http://alancalder.blogspot.com

Herbert Smith
www.herbertsmith.com

IT Governance Ltd (the company) and access to the online KnowledgeBank
www.itgovernance.co.uk

MICROSOFT

www.microsoft.com
www.microsoft.com/technet/default.asp
www.microsoft.com/downloads

Microsoft Security Centre
www.microsoft.com/technet/security/default.mspx

INFORMATION SECURITY

(UK) Alliance against Counterfeiting and Piracy
www.aacp.org.uk

Anti-phishing Working Group
www.antiphishing.org

British Computer Society
www.bcs.org

BSI
www.bsi-global.com

Bugtraq
www.securityfocus.com/archive/1

Carnegie Mellon Software Engineering Institute Computer Emergency
Response Team (CERT) Coordination Centre
www.cert.org

Center for Internet Security (CIS)
www.cisecurity.org

Common Criteria Portal
www.commoncriteriaportal.org

Common Vulnerabilities and Exposures
www.cve.mitre.org

(UK) Communications – Electronics Security Group
www.cesg.gov

Communications Security Establishment
www.cse-cst.gc.ca

Computer Security Institute
www.gocsi.com

Computer Security Online
www.compseconline.com

Computer Security Resource Clearinghouse (US National Institute of
Standards and Technology)
http://csrc.nist.gov

Ernst & Young e-security portal
www.esecurityonline.com

(UK) Federation Against Software Theft
www.fast.org.uk

GCHQ, Cheltenham
www.gchq.gov.uk

GIAC
www.giac.org

Information Commissioner
www.informationcommissioner.gov.uk

(UK) INFOSEC Exhibition
www.infosec.co.uk

International Computer Security Association
www.truesecure.com

International Information Systems Security Certification Consortium
www.isc2.org

Internet Security Alliance
www.isalliance.org

Internet Storm Center
http://isc.sans.org

(US) National Infrastructure Protection Centre
www.nipc.gov

(UK) National Infrastructure Security Co-ordination Centre
www.nisc.gov.uk

Open Web Application Security Project
www.owasp.org

(UK) Patent Office
www.patent.gov.uk

The SANS Institute
www.sans.org

The Virus Bulletin
www.virusbtn.com

OTHER

Business Continuity Information Centre
www.businesscontinuityworld.com

Carnegie Mellon Software Engineering Institute
www.sei.cmu.edu

CIO Magazine
www.cio.com

Computerworld Magazine
www.computerworld.com

(UK) Criminal Records Bureau
www.crb.gov.uk

(UK) Department of Trade and Industry
www.dti.gov.uk

Disaster Recovery Information Exchange
www.drie.org

Disaster Recovery Journal
www.drj.com

Disaster Resource Guide Online
www.disaster-resource.com

(UK) Financial Services Authority
www.fsa.gov.uk

Information Security Magazine
www.infosecuritymag.com

Information Week Online
www.informationweek.com

Institute of Chartered Accountants of England and Wales
www.icaew.co.uk

Institute of Directors
www.iod.com

The Internet Engineering Task Force (IETF)
www.ietf.org

Internet Watch Foundation
www.iwf.org.uk

The Open Source Initiative
www.opensource.org

The Risk Institute – Risk Management Resource Centre
www.riskinstitute.org

TickIT
www.tickit.org

WiFi Alliance
www.wi-fi.org

Index

NB: page numbers in *italic* indicate figures